Praise for

SURVIVING JONATHAN

"There's no algorithm for this kind of resilience. You either lived it or you didn't. Jonathan did. Every page reads like a man dragging wisdom out of the fire."

KATHERINE FOWLER, data scientist

"Jonathan has demonstrated a remarkable ability to navigate challenges and drive transformation."

ABC NEWS

"This book isn't just a read—it's a reckoning. Each chapter felt like it was written from the inside out. If you've ever felt lost, this is your map home."

DR. ORLANDO SKELTON, chief performance and executive intelligence advisor

"360 Degrees of Resilience provides unique insight into building resilient individuals."

YAHOO! FINANCE

"This book will meet you where you hurt. Jonathan proved that we can bend without breaking. Strength can live in even the most wounded parts of us."

CONSTANCE KNIGHT, head of content partnerships, Americas

"One book that is set to provide clarity during these confusing times is *Surviving Jonathan*."

NBC NEWS

"We say we want authentic leaders. A story like this shows up and reminds us what authenticity actually costs."

RODNEY TIDWELL, respiratory therapist, Providence

"Anyone who has faced chaos will see themselves in these pages. And for those who haven't, this unforgettable story is one you'll be glad you read."

SHERI BYERS, accountant and author

"This visionary book focuses on the importance of intentional resilience."

FOX NEWS

amplify
an imprint of Amplify Publishing Group

www.amplifypublishinggroup.com

Surviving Jonathan: The 360 Degrees of Resilience

This book is a work of non-fiction. It is based on the author's memories, experiences, and reflections. Some names, identifying details, and timelines have been changed or condensed to protect privacy. While efforts have been made to ensure accuracy, certain events have been re-created from memory and may contain unintentional inaccuracies or interpretations.

The content of this book may include discussions of sensitive topics such as trauma, addiction, and mental health. It is not intended to serve as medical, psychological, legal, or professional advice. Readers seeking guidance in any of these areas should consult with qualified professionals.

The views and opinions expressed are those of the author and do not represent those of any individuals or organizations mentioned.

For more information, please contact:
Amplify Publishing, an imprint of Amplify Publishing Group
620 Herndon Parkway, Suite 220
Herndon, VA 20170
info@amplifypublishing.com

Library of Congress Control Number: 2024919337

CPSIA Code: PRV0825A

ISBN-13: 979-8-89138-165-0

Printed in the United States

There is no better person to dedicate this book to than the little boy who still lives within me. Thank you for holding the weight until I was able to see you the way you needed to be seen. This book is your voice, your mic drop, and your confirmation that I now carry the weight of us to set you free.

SURVIVING JONATHAN

THE 360 DEGREES OF RESILIENCE

JONATHAN CRAWFORD

amplify
an imprint of Amplify Publishing Group

CONTENTS

PART II: RECKONING—BREAK WHAT'S BEEN BREAKING YOU

PART III: THE SHIFT—WHERE MOMENTUM IS BORN

PART IV: RISE—NO APOLOGIES. NO MASK. JUST RISE.

INTRODUCTION

I didn't set out to write a book. I set out to understand my life.

For years, I carried the weight of a story I wasn't sure I was ready to tell. Not because it wasn't worth telling, but because living it was hard enough. But over time, I started to see the patterns, the pain, the breakthroughs, and the quiet strength of resilience that kept me standing when everything else around me was falling apart.

I realized I wasn't just surviving. I was being shaped. And maybe someone out there needed the truth I used to hide. Maybe someone needed to know they weren't alone in their trauma, their rebuilding, or their search for meaning. So I wrote this book, not to showcase how far I've come but to share what it really took to get here.

Trauma wasn't new; it had already been riding shotgun most of my life. But when the crack era exploded, it got louder, darker, and more dangerous. My community and I weren't just fighting the streets—we were fighting the damage we carried inside. The unhealed wounds of our parents, the weight of fatherlessness, generational cycles, addiction, and abuse ... these weren't just issues—they were the atmosphere.

Life seemed poised to plunge me into self-destruction. Surrender would have been the easier option when facing such profound adversity. But somewhere between inherited pain and present chaos, I found a choice: either become another chapter in a generational story of loss, or rewrite the ending myself.

This defiance marked the beginning of my post-traumatic growth (PTG), a transformative journey through my trauma. I began to recognize and harness the lessons embedded in my hardships. This transformative process involved confronting and reframing my past experiences, allowing me to see them not just as sources of pain, but also as catalysts for personal development and empowerment.

Through this process, I learned the many dimensions of resilience embedded in my struggles, seeing them as opportunities for growth rather than mere obstacles. Unpacking those experiences in real time, alongside a future-focused mindset, helped me reconstruct my identity and start the work of healing and self-discovery.

I didn't take a traditional path into the business world of suits, systems, and politics. But I brought everything I had: the pressure-tested instincts, the hunger to prove myself, and the emotional intelligence sharpened by survival.

Each hurdle I overcame not only strengthened me but also enriched my understanding. Every success fueled my ambition. Today, I stand not as someone who figured it all out, but as someone who fought to become who I needed most. My story isn't polished, but it's real. And that's what makes it powerful.

This book isn't about recognition—it's about responsibility. For years, I searched for my greater purpose, knowing that the pain, growth, and resilience I fought for might help someone else fight their own way through.

This isn't a clean success story. And it's not just a personal story—it's a human one. It's what happens when survival stops being enough, and you decide to take your life back, piece by piece, choice by choice.

Whether you're navigating trauma, transition, leadership, or loss, this book is here to meet you where you are.

PART I

DESCENT—WHERE SURVIVAL BEGINS

Before I ever fought to live, I learned how to survive silence, shame, and shit no kid should ever carry.

1

HOW DID I GET HERE?

It was March 1987. I was twenty-three years old, and for two and a half years, I'd been addicted to smoking primos, a joint mixed with marijuana and crack cocaine. By now, every time I got high, all I felt was guilt. Guilt because I knew it was wrong. Guilt because I knew what it was doing to those in my life. Guilt because I knew this was not who I was supposed to be. At this point I'd been in and out of rehab many times. I failed to use the tools I'd learned to combat my urges time and time again. This day my wife was on my case *and* on her last straw. It had only been eight months since I'd begged her to leave me and take the kids. "Run!" I'd told her. "Get the hell out of here before I ruin your lives too!" After all the stress I had put her through and the sacrifices she had made, she continued to stand by me. Tonight, though, things were different. Maybe this time there would be no coming back. She'd had enough, and she had every right to feel this way.

My guilt was at an all-time high on this day. No pun intended. While my better half was at work, trying to hold our life together, I was home, primo in hand. She was *furious*. "How do I get out of this?" I asked myself. I had exhausted every trick in the book. My wonderful, demented mind told me the only way out of this was suicide. Yes, suicide. This was something I'd contemplated several times before but was never ballsy enough to do. But I needed a way out of this fight. My mind was swirling. *Is this something I can do? If so, how?* I didn't own a gun, and Lord knows I didn't have the guts to shoot myself. I could jump. But wait, our apartment was only two stories, so at most I would break an arm or leg. Plus I was afraid of heights.

As my wife continued to threaten to leave me, I told her I didn't want to live anymore. In that moment I meant it. I was ready to take my life. End it for good. She stared at me. If she was taken aback by my confession, she didn't show it. "Do it," she said. "I wish you would—save us all." *A challenge,* I thought. "Okay. I'll show you." It was time to play the victim, a role I had mastered since the start of my addiction. I stood and headed to the bedroom. I remembered I had a bottle of Halcion, a strong sleeping pill, on top of my dresser. I grabbed the pill bottle and made my way back down the hall to make a show of it. My mind was racing. *Are you really going to do this shit, Jonathan?* There was no turning back now. I had to call her bluff and show her she was wrong for telling me to do it. I wasn't taking any accountability for how I got here. I twisted the cap off, dumped a handful of pills into my hand, and slowly put them in my mouth, my heart pumping fast as I stared at her the whole time. I heard nothing from her as I walked away. Within minutes, I was woozy. When I fell to the ground, I knew she was finally worried. I could hear her going crazy, asking herself what she should do. I could hear her pleading for help to the woman across the hall. Our neighbor helped carry me downstairs and put me in the car. My wife then sped to the nearest emergency room. What a saint, that woman.

Somewhat lucid, I was placed on a gurney once we arrived at the ER. The medical staff rushed me into a room. My blood pressure was low. They were waving smelling salt under my nose, trying to keep me awake while simultaneously placing a needle in my arm to start an IV. I could hear the nurse: "Stay with us, Jonathan . . . Drink this." Not knowing what it was, I started to spit it out. Black liquid was dribbling down my chin and neck, staining my clothes. "It's charcoal, Jonathan," I heard the nurse say. But she sounded far away. It *was* charcoal that was being poured down my throat—activated charcoal. This method is sometimes used as an alternative to pumping someone's stomach. The chaos around me finally settled, and I was left in my room. The only sounds were the steady beeping of the machine I was hooked up to and the rigid breathing of my wife, who sat in the corner staring off into oblivion in disbelief.

I lay there for what seemed like a lifetime, contemplating my choices up to this point, when out of nowhere, I felt this sharp, constricting pain in my lower abdomen. Lurching upright in bed, I wrapped my arms around my cramping torso. My stomach started bubbling, and I knew the charcoal they'd given me was working overtime. "Nurse! Nurse!" I screamed as I attempted to push the call button while holding myself. My wife stared at me from her corner, mouth agape, not sure if she should intervene. One of the staff members finally came in, and before they finished pulling back the curtain, I was pleading to use the bathroom. I knew if I didn't make it in the next few seconds, shit was going to be everywhere—and I mean *everywhere*. The anguish on my face told the nurse everything she needed to know. She and a fellow coworker hustled me out of the bed and got me to the bathroom in the blink of an eye. Once the door closed, I uncovered my ass and let loose. I have never felt such a gratifying and horrific release as I did in that moment. Everything I had eaten over the past three days was pouring out of me. I swear you could hear me throughout the entire ER. I thought I was going to die sitting on that toilet. But when my body finally stopped contracting, I stood and turned to look at the damage I'd caused. My stool was pitch black. And it would have scared the shit out of me, but I had none left.

I returned to my room with the ER doctor and a psychiatrist waiting to see me. I must have been a sight because they stared at me for a long moment before saying a word. The psychiatrist introduced himself and asked all the standard questions: How are you feeling? Why did you feel the need to hurt yourself? Do you *want* help? Will you *let* us help? I answered all their questions as I watched my wife out of the corner of my eye. She was glaring at me. Hard. The look on her face was telling me, "If you say no, don't worry about coming home." But I wanted to go home. "Yes, Doc, I want help." I played the victim well, and as one, I had to see this act through to the end.

The doctor looked at me, his gaze assessing, and he made no effort to hide his skepticism. I could only imagine how many crackheads he'd tried to help before me. "We only have one bed for tonight in the psychiatric ward," he started. "This part of the unit stays locked, but we can move you tomorrow to the open unit. Are you willing to take the bed?" I didn't reply right away. The words "lock" and "psych ward" kept repeating in my head. "Can I come back tomorrow?" I stuttered. I could hear my wife muttering under her breath. I tried not to look at her. I knew my only option for a decent bed tonight would be here. "It's best you do not leave tonight," he replied. All I could muster was a defeated nod. I was scared.

After signing the admission papers, my wife left for the night. I gave her a subtle wave as they put me into a wheelchair. Her contemptuous expression said it all. She had had enough. So up the elevator I went, to the top floor—the *locked* unit of the psychiatric ward. We stopped at a door with a glass window, and from there we were buzzed in. The nurse's station sat behind thick glass. My first thought was that this was a jail—a jail without bars. I was shown around and taken to my room. They gave me a new gown so I could shower, which I needed desperately. My sweat-stained body reeked of drugs, and my gown had more than just charcoal stains on the back side after the multiple dumps I had taken, not to mention the numerous close calls.

I tried to settle in, but I needed food. Everything I had eaten in the past few days was gone. My whole system was flushed clean. The staff kindly offered me a sandwich from the refrigerator, and I was grateful. But once I made it back to my room, that fear started setting in again. My roommate was making unnerving sounds and talking to himself. I couldn't quite make out what he was saying, and I didn't ask. At this point I was just tired as hell, so I lay down on my cot. The lights were out; it was pitch black. As soon as I felt sleep start to take over, my eyes bolted back open. "What did you say?" I asked out loud as my roommate paced the floor. I thought he was talking to me, but he was just walking around the room in the dark, humming and having multiple conversations with all his personalities. At that point my heart was racing, but I lay back down. No matter what he said, I kept my mouth shut and eyes open. All I could think was, *What the hell have you done, Jonathan?* This was one high that wasn't worth it.

As the night continued, he went to sleep. Finally, I could take my ass to sleep and pray for morning to come, or so I thought. Around two in the morning, as the hallway light beamed into our room from the little square window in the door, I could see the guy attempting to read my paperwork in the dark. I just lay there in fear. I didn't dare breathe. I didn't know what he was capable of. But right then and there, I knew I was in the wrong place. How did I get here? How could I let myself get here? Without warning he threw himself at the door and banged his head against the window, again and again and again. He didn't realize that the door was unlocked, and he could just walk out. All he had to do was pull the handle. I was still lying there, bug-eyed. "What the fuck, man!" I unknowingly shouted. Realizing my mistake, I quickly clapped my hands over my mouth, but it was too late.

My roommate stopped and slowly turned toward my bed. I could see blood trickling down his head from where he had been hitting it. The vacant look on his face only added to his menacing demeanor as he approached my bed. And then he just fell on top of me. Man, I jumped so far out of that bed, you would have thought I sprouted wings. My feet hit the floor without my butt ever sliding across the mattress. I was ready to knock his ass out until I realized the condition he was in. I went to the door and yelled for a nurse. Given the hour, they rushed into the room and medicated him so he could sleep—so I could sleep. Later, I found out he was on lithium and Haldol, two very powerful drugs to treat mental disorders.

I lay there for the rest of the night, unable to sleep. I felt guilty and sad for what I had put my wife through, but mostly for what I had put myself through. I found myself crying for the way I was treating this little boy inside me. The child who only had me to depend on all his life. Who relied on me to keep him safe. Now look at what I was doing to him. I was his worst enemy. My mind was running with fear, and all I thought throughout the night was, *How did I get here? How did I get here? Jonathan, how did you get here?*

2

BACK IN THE DAY

When I was just seven years old, I wanted to join a gang. The LA street gang scene was in its infancy at the time. Well-known gangs such as the Crips, which originally started out as a neighborhood watch group, became more immersed in criminal activity, resulting in the formation of one of the most notorious street gangs. The Bloods emerged as a rival to the Crips in the early 1970s, resulting in one of the most well-known rivalries in gang history. Other gangs such as Mara Salvatrucha (MS-13), the Avenues, 18th Street Gang, and Black Guerrilla Family (BGF) were scattered throughout the Los Angeles area and were often associated with the rampant crime, violence, and drug trafficking that plagued my youth and young adulthood. But at seven I didn't know any of this. Gang life seemed like security, something I had been sorely lacking since I was about five years old. Ultimately, I knew gang life wasn't for me when I found out that the initiation process started with having to fight the toughest member in the gang, and all other members had the option to jump in and beat me. I quickly thought, the hell with that shit!

A few years later, my mom moved my siblings and me to a better neighborhood. However, within four or five years, my new neighborhood started to change. The shift in atmosphere felt like going from a beautiful, breezy spring day to a harsh, unrelenting winter—a winter that persisted for decades. My unhurried stroll to school soon became rushed with me constantly looking over my shoulder. When I was eleven, my skateboard was stolen, ripped right out of my hands. Walking home, I remember thinking, *Why would someone take something that means so much to me when I already have so little?* I cried all the way home that day. Just a few years later, at thirteen, my bike was snatched by a grown-ass man. This time I resisted, but he overpowered me and threw me to the ground. "Don't make me hurt you, kid. I'll kick your ass." And with that he rode away. That bike was my only means of transportation. Without it I had a ten-mile walk to school because the transit buses were on a five-month strike, and we had no car.

I was fortunate not to become a statistic to gang violence, especially after experiencing so many close calls. One of the first occurred when I was about fifteen. One night my mother sent me to the store with a note giving them permission to sell me a pack of cigarettes. In those days a note went a long way. It read, "To Whom It May Concern, you have my permission to sell my son, Jonathan Crawford, two packs of Marlboro cigarettes. If you have any problems, you may call me at xxx-xxxx. Thank you. His mother, Earnestine." I remember feeling especially irritated that I had to run this errand. That evening I came across a handful of gang members shooting dice across the street. Since I knew everyone in the neighborhood, I felt safe. So after a few pleasantries between us, I made my way to the end of the block, preparing to cross the street.

As I began to step off the curb, a car pulled up in front of me with its lights off. When I stopped, they shouted past me, "What set is this, cuz?" The gang members down the block responded, "Blood!" Frozen in place, I went from a block of ice to a ball of fire as a shotgun barrel emerged from the car window. Instinctively, I dove between parked cars just moments before gunfire erupted. As the shotgun discharged, the gang members on my street retaliated, rushing toward the opposing gang. I lay there, hands over my head, shaking like a California earthquake. When the gunfire ceased, I ran my ass home. My mom was standing outside, frantically calling my name. She hugged me as I bolted into the house. In a mix of relief and frustration, I tossed the note on the floor, contemplating how I had almost lost my life over cigarettes I didn't even smoke.

Some years later my friend Dave came over, and as night fell, we left my place to walk to his house. We only lived about five blocks apart. As we turned onto his block and passed a few houses, we noticed five boys riding their bikes across the street. They were yelling at us to come over. Choosing to ignore them, we kept walking. A few seconds later, I glanced over and saw one of them had a gun in his hand. To this day I'm uncertain what prompted me to look and how I spotted the weapon on that dark street. Maybe it was just my sixth sense I'd developed or some innate survival instinct I'd honed over the years.

Immediately, I shouted to Dave, "Gun!" We dove behind the only parked car on his block, quickly realizing it was not a safe place to stay. Despite the tight jeans of the 1970s and the cowboy boots I had decided to wear, I sprinted toward Dave's house, and he followed suit. Gunfire chased us—a rapid series of pops that seemed unending. Turning toward a tree in Dave's front yard, I let my intuition guide me to fall and roll. I dropped to the ground, and with the momentum of my chaotic run, I quickly stood back up without missing a stride—my boots transforming into makeshift track shoes.

As the shooting ceased, the small gang of boys began to make their escape. Fueled by adrenaline, I frantically checked my body for wounds, unsure if I had been shot. Thankfully, to my surprise and by the grace of God, they had missed. Unfortunately, the same could not be said for Dave. Entering the house, he realized he was bleeding; a bullet had passed through his hand. Dave's dad, a pharmacist, rushed to his side. Despite hearing the shots, he hadn't realized we were the targets. Dave, in pain and screaming, swallowed two pain pills his dad gave him, and we rushed him to the emergency room. This was the most frightening moment of my life.

Consequently, the culmination of these life-threatening and traumatic childhood ordeals proved to be life-altering. One evening I was on the bus, returning home from my after-school job at Jack in the Box. As the bus neared my stop, I stood and moved toward the front when a loud boom echoed. This was likely from a car backfiring. Instinctively, I dove to the bus floor, lying in the aisle with my hands shielding my head. After a few tense seconds, I stood, only to find everyone on the bus staring at me, some even laughing. The embarrassment and fear were evident on my face. Leaving the bus, I was shaken, and I began running the six blocks home as fast as I could, tears streaming down my face. In that moment I felt no different from a war veteran, grappling with PTSD from the perilous streets of South Central LA. To this day I still find myself looking over my shoulder and sitting with my back against a wall.

3

THE BURDEN WE CAN'T SEE

"You're the man of the house now." I was ten years old when my mother said this to me. My older brother had just left for the military, and because I was next in line, the responsibility was thrust upon me. But what did that even mean—*being the man of the house*? How was I supposed to know what that looked like when I had no example? I didn't have a father in the house to show me. There were no lessons passed down. I was just a kid, suddenly expected to fill shoes I had never even seen walked in. So I did what I thought men were supposed to do—work, provide, and carry everything without complaint. But looking back, I wasn't becoming a man. I was just a child *pretending* to be one.

If my family structure sounds complicated, that's because it was. My mom had four children from a previous marriage before having three kids with my father. I was the first of those three. My father, on the other hand, had one child from his first marriage, three with my mother, and three with my first stepmother. I was number two of his seven. The problem? His kids, including me, were the result of a back-and-forth between our moms.

That meant I had some siblings born in the same year. Imagine trying to wrap your head around that as a kid. I spent years confused as hell, constantly trying to figure out what the fuck was going on. Who belonged where? Who was full-blooded, half, or step? I didn't even have the language to describe it, just this feeling that I was supposed to understand something that made no sense.

On top of that, the absence of my father would go on to create a father wound* that affected me for years. It's not that we didn't spend time together—I did see him. But it was always me initiating that time, always me asking if I could come over. I wanted that connection, and I fought for it. But there's something about being the kid who always has to ask for time from a parent that makes you feel like maybe you're not important enough to be given it freely.

I was lucky, though. My first stepmother, the one my father had three kids with, cared deeply for all his children, even the ones who weren't hers. That gave me a sense of comfort that I didn't even realize I was looking for.

At the age of thirteen, I was thrust into the role of parentification, also known as a parentified child—where a child or adolescent is obliged to support the family system in ways that are developmentally inappropriate and overly burdensome. There's a term for it now, but back then it was just life. The weight of responsibility

---

* **The father wound** is the internal injury created when a father is physically absent, emotionally distant, abusive, or simply unable to provide the love, protection, validation, or guidance a child needs. It can shape one's identity, relationships, self-worth, and worldview long into adulthood.

Important distinction: *A father wound doesn't require a cruel or malicious father. Sometimes it comes from a father who was doing his best—but whose own limitations, trauma, or emotional unavailability still left a lasting mark.*

forced me to mature faster than my peers, but it came at a cost: my childhood.

While I desired to help my family, I also wanted to just be a kid without the weight of the world on my shoulders. Balancing my own emotional needs with the responsibilities on my shoulders was an ongoing struggle. I had to figure out how to process pain, disappointment, and frustration on my own. There was no safe space to unload my feelings, no one to guide me through what I was experiencing. I learned to suppress emotions rather than express them because showing vulnerability wasn't an option. If I broke down, who was going to put me back together? So I internalized everything—turning pain into silence, frustration into drive, and loneliness into resilience. But the weight of carrying all that, at such a young age, was something I didn't fully understand until much later in life.

Since the age of fourteen, I worked multiple jobs. My very first job was through the city of LA's summer work program, picking up trash at local parks. I worked five hours a day, Monday through Friday. And let me tell you, Mondays were the worst. The weekend crowds left behind mountains of trash, and by the time we clocked in, the parks looked like an explosion of fast-food wrappers, beer cans, condoms, and cigarette butts. It was nasty work, but I didn't complain because that paycheck was my first real taste of independence.

After my summer job, I started working at Jack in the Box. They put me on the fryer at first, but within six months I could run an entire shift. I learned quickly and took on extra responsibilities, and before long they were eyeing me for a shift manager position at just seventeen.

That would have been a big deal—a teenager managing an entire store. But before I could officially move up, a new manager came, and my hours got cut. That was it for me. If I couldn't work full-time, I wasn't staying, so I walked away. But looking back, that moment was more than just quitting a job; it was the beginning of a habit I would struggle with for years. Every time I faced a setback or felt unappreciated, my instinct was to leave. Instead of pushing through disappointment, I let frustration dictate my decisions. Leaving felt easier than staying. Walking away meant I controlled the disappointment before it could control me. It was survival, not failure. This pattern would follow me, showing up in ways I didn't fully recognize until much later in life.

During my senior year of high school, I landed a telemarketing job selling ink for copy machines. This wasn't flipping burgers or picking up trash. This was sitting behind a desk, combing through leads, trying to convince people to buy something they probably didn't need. Some weeks, I made hundreds of dollars. Some weeks? Nothing. That's the nature of sales. The unpredictability of it was exhausting for a seventeen-year-old, but I had no choice. My jobs were out of necessity rather than choice.

But what I didn't realize at the time was that I was developing a skill that would become one of my greatest strengths—persuasion. I learned how to develop my voice to sell, to influence, to connect. That skill would follow me for the rest of my life.

Growing up in poverty meant wearing worn-out clothes, shopping in thrift stores, and enduring years with the same tattered tennis shoes. My earnings primarily covered personal necessities such as clothes, school lunches, and bus fare. Additionally, I regularly contributed to household expenses, acutely aware of the stress gripping my mother in our struggle to maintain a roof over our heads. Despite living in a disadvantaged neighborhood, I clung to the belief that my surroundings wouldn't define me; instead, they could fortify my determination for change.

Music became my primary outlet. Spending time alone, I found solace and a connection to the timeless tunes that seemed to echo the essence of an old soul. Certain lyrics, like those in Roberta Flack's "Killing Me Softly with His Song," had a profound emotional impact, bringing tears to my eyes when I was just an eight-year-old in third grade. I didn't understand why at the time, but something about the sadness in the melody and the haunting way she sang resonated deeply with me. Maybe it was the loneliness I carried, the feeling that no one saw me or understood me. The song felt like it knew a pain I couldn't yet put into words, and in that moment it was as if someone, somewhere, understood exactly how I felt.

Despite the unusualness of a child crying to a song, it marked a unique connection that I cherished. Music not only served as an emotional anchor but also provided a space where I could lose myself entirely. Throughout my journey from childhood to adolescence, music remained a constant source of joy and excitement. The albums I cherished then still hold a special place in my collection today. In my solitude I dreamed of becoming a radio DJ, spending hours mimicking broadcasts with the signature introduction, "Hey, this is Jonathan Crawford." It was a lit experience for me, a respite from the challenges surrounding my family and me. As I grew older, I became a different kind of DJ, a party DJ. Spinning records emerged as my passion and refuge, as well as a side hustle that helped make the money my family needed. At every party I played, my worries dissolved, offering a reprieve from witnessing my mom's constant concerns about bills and our family's ongoing struggles. But my real saving grace was always my self-motivation. I was a dreamer, envisioning my future self dressing purposefully even when I had nowhere to go. "Dress for the job you want, not the one you have, Jonathan," I'd tell myself. Existential questions haunted me: Who am I? Where am I heading? What should I do? Even if I find answers, how do I navigate my way there? I needed to confront the harsh reality that haunted many young African Americans—becoming a statistic in an impoverished neighborhood. Despite my empty pockets and lack of skills, I was determined to avoid ending up in jail or being lost to the system.

I needed a stable job, something that could create momentum. But where does a kid with no degree, no trade, and no road map even start? Every job listing felt like it was asking for something I didn't have. The world beyond minimum wage seemed locked behind doors I didn't have the key for.

Try this: Write down one burden you've been carrying since childhood. Who gave it to you? Why did you accept it?

Now ask: Is it still yours to carry?

4

OLD SOUL

People often referred to me as an "old soul." I owed this to my early development, perceptive nature, and a maturity level that far exceeded my age. Occasionally, I wondered whether my early exposure to adult indulgences such as alcohol and tobacco played a role in shaping my experiences. My first encounter with intoxication happened unexpectedly one Christmas morning when I was five. While joyfully riding my new little red fire truck around our home, I accidentally drank from a glass containing scotch and milk, which was sitting on the coffee table.

At first I didn't notice anything unusual, but soon I was crashing into furniture like a drunk driver. My mom, realizing that her cocktails were mysteriously disappearing, pulled me out of the fire truck and laughed as I staggered across the room, wobbling like a miniature old man on a binge. Later that day we left for my grandmother's house for Christmas dinner, but I was in no state to walk. They had to carry me inside, my head lolling against my uncle's shoulder. He chuckled and said, "That boy is feeling the way I want to feel!" My grandfather, aware of my condition, scooped me up in his arms, and I promptly peed on him. That was the last thing I remembered before being put to bed at five in the afternoon, sleeping straight through until the next morning.

At the age of seven, I shared a moment with my father, trying a tobacco pipe. I wanted to be like him, to do the things grown men did. Sitting with him while I puffed on that pipe gave me a sense of closeness, a fleeting moment where I felt like I belonged in his world. That is, until my dumb ass started choking on the smoke. It took my breath away, leaving me grasping at my throat like I had just swallowed fire. My dad patted my back, laughing while I wheezed, my tiny lungs betraying my attempt at manhood.

But I wasn't one to give up easily. A few months later, determined to redeem myself, I took my experimentation to the next level. I sneaked into the bathroom with a pack of my mom's cigarettes, lighting them one by one, convinced I was mastering the art of smoking. I felt like a king in my foggy little throne room, until my older brother Gregory saw smoke coming from under the door, and he burst in. The look on his face as he stepped into a thick cloud of smoke was priceless. I had completely forgotten about the lingering evidence. He coughed, eyes wide, and before I could even think of an excuse, he yelled, "Mom!" After the ass whipping, that was the last time I attempted to smoke as a kid.

By the time I was sixteen, I was drinking and allowed to do it openly at home. I would attend dance functions with my mom, where the music, the energy, and the freedom to drink only reinforced the idea that I was far beyond my years. It wasn't just about the alcohol; it was about feeling like an adult, seamlessly blending into a world I thought I was ready for.

As I transitioned into adulthood, I noticed a strong attraction toward older women, consistently dating those who were significantly more mature. My attraction wasn't just about their confidence and experience—it was also fueled by my growing sexual appetite.

I took pride in presenting myself as an older man, carefully curating my image to fit the part. I wore sport jackets that added a touch of sophistication and cowboy boots that gave me a rugged, mature edge and carried myself with the confidence of someone well beyond my years. I wasn't just mimicking adulthood—I was embodying it, adopting the mannerisms and presence of a gentleman, someone who could walk into a room and be taken seriously, despite my actual age. But the contrast between looking and acting older yet being completely directionless was something I couldn't ignore. I wanted to believe I had it all figured out, but there were moments when the facade cracked. Like the countless times I was treated like an adult—given privileges, taken seriously—while internally I still felt unprepared, like a kid playing dress-up in a world that expected me to have all the answers.

While I felt ahead of my years, it also created a disconnect. My friends weren't allowed to do the things I could. They weren't drinking at home or attending dance functions with their mothers, and they certainly weren't dating older women. While they navigated high school crushes and part-time jobs, I was moving in a completely different world—one where I had access to experiences they could only hear about in whispers. I found myself always searching—but for what? Was it safety, or was it the care and emotional support I lacked? The answers eluded me.

On October 22, 1983, a couple of friends invited me to attend a dance hosted by their father at his social club. For me, dancing was a bigger outlet than spinning records. I could dance for hours, and this continued throughout my life. It was the one thing that I could lose myself in completely. And even though I was shy as a kid, I could let it all go and dance in front of the world. Passionate about dancing, I enthusiastically agreed to go. I got dressed in jeans, cowboy boots, and a sport coat; picked up another buddy of mine; and hit the road. When we arrived, the place was packed. We found a table close to one full of women, but what I wanted was a dance partner. Man, I really enjoyed myself on that dance floor.

As the night went on, though, my eyes kept going back to a woman sitting directly behind me. She was a stunner. The first thing I noticed about her was her smile. It was warm and inviting. She immediately felt safe and like home. Despite our obvious age difference (at least to me), I couldn't resist asking her to dance. Summoning up my courage, I finally approached her and introduced myself. Her name was Melissa, and I was beside myself. We owned that dance floor for the rest of the night. As the party started to wind down, I joined her at her table, and we talked for what seemed like hours. When she asked about my age, I played along with her guessing game. She landed on twenty-five, and all I could do was nod in agreement. I asked her age, and she said, "Thirty-three." What a fool I was to think my lack of honesty would never catch up to me.

We discovered that we lived on the same street, one block away from each other. It felt as if we had known each other long before that night. Before parting ways, I mustered the courage to ask for her number, and then I headed home.

Over the next few months, we spent a lot of time together. I learned that she was divorced with two children, a thirteen-year-old son and an eight-year-old daughter. It didn't faze me one bit that I was only six years older than her son. My younger brother and sister also spent time with them, as they were close in age. The more time we spent together, the harder I fell. I was convinced that our fourteen-year age difference wasn't an issue. The original lie about my age? That was the issue. And the closer we became, the more anxious I was about telling her. My lie had become my big elephant in the room. It was unbearable, and the time came when I couldn't carry it any longer. It was time to bring this darkness into the light.

I called Melissa and invited her to come over. I was going to tell her. Though she lived close by, the clock seemed to stop as I waited for her. A wave of nerves gripped me as I paced the floor, my heart racing, my palms and underarms soaked with sweat. The moment she walked in, she knew something was wrong. It was written all over my face. In a panic she started guessing. Was there another woman? Did I get another woman pregnant? Was *she* the other woman? I assured her it was none of these, but I could tell her patience was wearing thin. She sat in the nearest chair, trying to compose herself. Summoning all my courage, I blurted out the truth. "I lied about my age," I admitted, my voice barely above a whisper. She blinked, her expression shifting from confusion and disbelief. "What do you mean you lied about your age? Are you older?" I swallowed hard. "No . . . I'm younger." Her eyes narrowed as she leaned in, her tone sharper now. "How much younger are you, Jonathan?" "I am only twenty years old." There was only silence.

In a wildly incoherent manner, I started professing my love. "I had no idea it would be this wonderful . . . no idea you would be . . . " I trailed off, looking down at my feet. I could feel her eyes on me, assessing me. In that moment I knew I looked like the boy I still was in many ways. "How old are you? Are you twenty now . . . or twenty when we met?" She posed a solid question. After all, we had just recently celebrated my birthday. It was Super Bowl weekend, and I had just sat down in front of my cake. "Hey, there are too many candles on the cake! Shouldn't it be twenty?" my friend Dave shouted from behind me. In a panic, I immediately yelled, "Twenty-six!" then turned and shot him a menacing look that said, "Shut the fuck up, man!" No one knew I was hiding my real age from Melissa, but the look I gave that day spoke for itself. I couldn't even pick up my head when I replied to her.

My stomach dropped. It was the moment I had been dreading, the one I had run from for months. I wanted to say something clever, to downplay it, but there was no talking my way out of this. I could see the calculation in her eyes, the weight of fourteen years between us settling in. I felt like a kid caught with his hand in the cookie jar, except the consequences weren't just a scolding; they were the possible loss of someone I had fallen for. My mouth went dry.

"I just turned twenty." I was hoping she'd hear the sorrow in my voice. "You mean you were only nineteen when we met?" she asked. I replied, "Yes." The room fell silent once again. She then stood, grabbed her purse, opened the front door, and walked out without uttering a single word.

Something told me that she felt the same way about me as I did her. This made the bomb I just dropped that much more devastating. My thoughts couldn't help but echo, over and over again, *You big-ass dummy!* Simultaneously, I pondered that had she known my actual age, our connection would have never happened. My only solace lay in the hope that my character and maturity would overshadow the age disparity and the lie.

Days passed, and I did everything I could to not go and bang on her front door. Just when I was ready to do just that, she called me. She said she needed the time to reflect on the situation. Fourteen years was a tough pill to swallow. She spoke of the hurt I had caused her, the challenge it posed with kids close to my age, and what her parents would say, but she couldn't deny her growing feelings for me. Conversations with her friends, particularly one, posed the crucial question, "Are you happy?" This led her to realize that age can be merely a number. I was filled with both excitement and relief. I couldn't believe the next words that came out of her mouth: "Jonathan, I forgive you." From that moment on, our relationship inspired me to seek more in my life.

Being labeled an old soul wasn't just a compliment; it became an expectation, a role I constantly felt I had to live up to. While it had its advantages, allowing me to navigate adult spaces with ease, command a certain level of respect, and move ahead faster than my peers, it also came with its struggles. It made me feel isolated from people my own age, disconnected from experiences I probably should have had. It forced me to project confidence in moments where I felt completely unprepared. More than anything, it made me believe I had to have everything figured out, even when deep down I was just a kid trying to keep up with the image others had created for me. In chasing that identity, I never stopped to ask myself if it was who I actually wanted to be.

5

THE BELLMAN

It's funny how life works. One moment you're carrying luggage, greeting strangers, and mastering the art of small talk. The next you're staring at the same hotel from the outside, wondering where it all went wrong. But before everything changed, before I lost myself, this was where I found my confidence for the first time.

At the age of twenty, my journey of self-discovery kicked off with my first significant job as a bellman and room service waiter for a hotel chain. My best friend Wayne, who also worked at the hotel, referred me for the job, and I quicky immersed myself into the role. This job became something more—a mirror reflecting my untapped potential, a proving ground where I learned the value of service, discipline, and, most importantly, confidence.

Wayne and I were the only two Black people working at the hotel, and stepping into this environment was eye-opening. It wasn't just about carrying bags and greeting guests; it was also about navigating a space where we had to prove ourselves in ways others didn't. I quickly realized that in this job, being personable and attentive would take me further than just showing up and doing the minimum. The smallest details mattered—remembering a guest's name, anticipating their needs, making them feel seen. And I was good at it.

But that didn't mean self-doubt didn't creep in. There were moments in the early days when I questioned whether I really belonged. On one of my first shifts, I dropped the food tray while making a room service delivery. All the dishes shattered into pieces. I was mortified. Wayne pulled me aside later and said, "Shake it off, man. You can do this." And I did. I learned that confidence wasn't about never making mistakes—it was about how you handled them.

My work ethic quickly set me apart. I showed up early, stayed late, and went beyond what was expected. Within months my diligence paid off with a promotion to front desk clerk. The uniform changed from the casual bellman khaki pants and polo shirt to a sharp, more formal sport jacket, slacks, and tie. That first day behind the front desk, I felt different—more official, like I had stepped into a new version of myself. This wasn't just a job anymore. It was also a chance to prove what I was capable of. I managed a cash drawer that started at $500 and grew to thousands by the end of my shifts. I learned the art of booking the hotel to capacity, securing early check-ins for VIPs, and handling the controlled chaos of a busy front desk.

Simultaneously, my personal life was thriving. After blissfully dating Melissa for nine months, I proposed, and we decided to marry the following summer. Navigating through this old soul persona, I've learned to shoulder responsibility. This led me to believe I was prepared for even greater responsibilities—a wife and two children at twenty. I told myself it was love. But it was also the emotional anchor I'd never had before. At twenty, love and stability can look a lot alike when you've spent most of your life without either. But either way, I was all in.

A new promotion, a fiancée, and a fresh car—my blue 1984 Nissan SX hatchback, which had just replaced my reliable but aging 1966 Ford Fairlane—all within thirty days. I felt unstoppable. But looking back, I wonder if I mistook movement for progress, stability for purpose.

I wish I could say I saw what was coming. That I knew the momentum of this success wouldn't last. But at the time I was focused on climbing, on pushing forward, on proving something—maybe to myself, maybe to the world.

I had no idea that this very hotel, the place that had given me confidence and a sense of direction, would also become the setting of my greatest struggles in life. But that part of the story was still waiting for me down the short road ahead.

For now I was just a young man, standing at the front desk in a crisp suit, believing I had finally found my place.

6

SWEET MIRIAN

I should have known. I should have caught it. I should have stopped her. But I didn't. A gun. A single gun changed everything. It wasn't mine. It wasn't hers. But it still took her life. And now all I had left were questions—and rage.

Despite having three older sisters and an older brother in the house, Mirian was the closest in age to me until my younger brother was born. She was six years older. She was the quiet one—reserved and incredibly caring. There was a softness to her, an unshakable kindness that radiated through her eyes, and she was always attentive toward me.

While I lacked very few direct male role models in my life, Mirian was a different kind of role model. A nurturer. Even though my mother was quite present, there was always a wall around her that no one, not even her children, could penetrate. And while she was very quick to hug me that night when I was sent out to retrieve her cigarettes, those moments were few and far between. But in my eyes, Mirian seemed to be the heart of our family. She was my heart.

Our close relationship began when I was in kindergarten and she was in sixth grade. She was responsible for walking me home every day. That mile-long journey hand in hand meant everything to me. It wasn't just a walk—it was also a moment of safety, of belonging. Even as I grew older, she remained my protector. Throughout my teens she taught me how to present myself and how to dress. She braided my hair, complimented my appearance, and ensured I knew I was somebody. She believed in me in a way that I struggled to believe in myself. Our connection was unparalleled; we rarely fought during our childhood, unlike some of my other siblings.

Mirian was brilliant. Her humility and creativity left a lasting impression, and there was nothing better than seeing her smile and hearing her call my name. She was an incredible artist who could not be ignored. I remember she was always entering art contests, and once she won a nationwide competition, earning her second place and a college scholarship. By the age of twenty-two, she had an established career as a mechanical draftsman, drawing designs for top secret projects for the US government. Whenever I asked her about it, she'd always say, "You know, John, most of the time, I don't even know what I'm drawing." And then she'd laugh that bubbly laugh of hers. Nothing short of amazing, Mirian was also the only female and African American in her top classified department at the now-defunct Hughes Aerospace. But none of that intimidated her. If anything, she carried her uniqueness like a badge of honor. One of the most important lessons she taught me was that *you can chase your dreams, and with hard work, you can catch them.*

Mirian and I never said goodbye to each other. It was always "See you later." This fact should seem insignificant. And up until the day Mirian took her own life, I thought it was.

It was August 7, 1984, and Mirian asked me to join her for lunch before my swing shift. Spending over an hour together, we delved into discussions about her family, touched upon her police officer husband, Michael, their twenty-one-month-old son, and her admiration for me. Her encouragement regarding my future and the value of hard work left an enduring impression. Our lunch concluded with a heartening expression of love and pride in my accomplishments. Carrying her words with me, I headed to work with a joyous spirit. The conversation lingered in my thoughts throughout the day, cementing our adult relationship.

At five o'clock the next morning, the phone rang. The sound of it sent a shiver down my spine before I even answered. My mother's voice was frantic, screaming into the receiver, "Jonathan! Jonathan! Jonathan!" I frantically replied, "Mom, what's wrong?" She urgently said, *"Mirian shot herself in the head! Get to the hospital!"* I sat there in bed, frozen, unwilling to accept what I was hearing. I lingered before I got up, unprepared for the profound changes that loomed as I stepped out. When I arrived at the hospital, my mother and brother Gregory greeted me with sorrowful expressions. The crushing truth unfolded—my sister, my confidante, my heart had shot herself in the head, taking her own life. In that moment I was broken forever. I stood in shock, desperately clinging to any hope that it was just a nightmare.

The hospital staff consoled us and offered to take us to see her. We all crammed into the elevator, up to the third floor. No one spoke or dared to even breathe as the elevator ascended. The truth hit us as soon as those doors opened. Waves and waves of distraught cries echoed around us. As I looked around the room, I noticed it was all Michael's family, crying over my sister as if they had lost a sister, a daughter, a mother. Mirian was gone. It *was* true. My mother fainted the moment we stepped onto the third floor, her body crumpling beneath the weight of the grief. Gregory and I barely caught her before she hit the floor. The nurses rushed to help, but the damage was already done. As I tried to console my mom, anger swelled within me, mixing with my grief and engulfing me. How did they fucking know before us? Why were we kept in the dark? Where the fuck was my brother-in-law? Where the fuck was Michael?

Returning to the ground floor, I saw Melissa waiting. The second our eyes met, I felt the weight of the words I had to say crush me. My mouth opened, but no sound came out at first. Then I forced it out. "Mirian is gone. Melissa, she is gone." And I cried. Over and over again, I cried.

Melissa's face twisted, her lips trembling as she tried to process what I had just said. I watched as the reality hit her, the disbelief in her eyes shattering into sorrow. My words hung in the air like a death sentence, heavy and inescapable. The moment stretched endlessly between us, and I realized there was no way to make this easier. No way to soften it. No way to bring her back. I felt the ground beneath me shift, like I was watching my own life from outside my body. My chest swelled, and my fists clenched. The harsh reality wasn't just difficult to digest—it was unbearable.

I had known Michael since the age of twelve. He and Mirian were high school sweethearts. He was like another brother to me. But despite my close bond with him, I needed someone to blame. I became fixated on blaming my brother-in-law. It was almost a psychopathic obsession. It fueled an irrational need for vengeance, because without it to focus on, all that would be left was pain.

After speaking with the Inglewood police department detective, I would learn over the next few days that Mirian had shot herself with Michael's police-issued gun. He wasn't at the hospital because he was being questioned at the police station trying to explain what had happened. He was there, and it was rumored he tried to stop her. But I wasn't there. I didn't see it. I never got to hear his side, only the pieces my family gave me. And even that remained unclear. The weight of that gun, the authority it represented, had turned into something unspeakable. It wasn't just a weapon; it had become a permanent wound in all our lives.

Some family members alluded to marital problems, Mirian's depression, and her possible crack use. I didn't believe a single word of it. I *knew* Mirian. She was happy and bubbly and full of life. Wasn't she?

I thought about our last lunch together. She couldn't stop telling me how proud she was of me. She told me to take care of Melissa and myself. "You better treat her right, John. I am proud of you." Then she said goodbye. Mirian never said goodbye. Not to me. Not to anyone. Because goodbye meant something was final. It meant no more jokes, no more hair braiding, no more "John, you know you're handsome, right?" It meant no more Mirian. But that day, she said it. She looked me in the eyes, smiled that warm, knowing smile of hers, and said, "Goodbye, John. You take good care of yourself, and remember, I love you." And I didn't even realize what she was telling me.

This only made the pain that much greater. Her coming to praise me left me questioning whether she had said this for me or herself. This was something I would never be able to reconcile.

If you are grieving, try this: Say their name. Out loud. Write a letter, a poem, or even just a sentence to someone you've lost. Don't worry about closure—just honor the connection.

7

SINKING

Grief doesn't just sink you; it drowns you. And the night I lost my sister, I was willing to let it.

On the night of my sister's passing, my friends were aware of my pain. They stopped by, sensing the weight I was carrying. I let them in, hoping their presence might lighten some of it. We exchanged hugs, murmured condolences, and settled into the kind of silence that only grief can command.

Seeking solace, one of them brought along some cognac, and we began pouring drinks. The desire for the fiery warmth of alcohol was strong that night, and I craved its numbing effect. Alongside the drinks, we turned to my usual escape—smoking weed. The familiar haze wrapped around me, offering a fleeting sense of calm, a brief moment when grief loosened its grip.

As the night unfolded, one of my friends proposed trying something different—a "primo." The moment the word left his mouth, something inside me hesitated, but I shoved it down. I wasn't thinking straight. I wasn't thinking at all. I was drowning, and if this could dull the pain faster, why the hell not? I just lost my sister. What else could I lose? Curious, I asked what it was. They explained it was a mix of weed and rock cocaine, a stronger, faster high that hit differently. While I had heard of rock cocaine and its addictiveness, I was unfamiliar with its effects, especially when combined with weed. However, in my desperate attempt to dull the pain, I was open to anything that promised relief. The primo was rolled and ignited, and its distinct aroma filled the air. It had a sharpness to it, a chemical bitterness that cut through the usual earthy scent of weed. Something about it felt unnatural, but I took the hit anyway.

The smoke burned differently, clinging to my lungs in a way I wasn't used to. Later on this smell would be one of my greatest triggers—the kind that made my mouth water. But this first time, as it was passed to me, I took a deep drag and held the smoke within for a few seconds before exhaling slowly. A cloud of smoke billowed in front of my face. The rush hit me like a lightning bolt—sudden and electric. It was unlike anything I had experienced before. It was intense and transformative. My body felt weightless, and my mind was floating somewhere beyond the walls of the room. Momentarily, the anguish of losing my sister disappeared. I told myself it was nothing. Just one time. Just for tonight. But even in that moment, a whisper of something dark settled in my gut. A seed had been planted, and I didn't even realize it.

I continued to indulge in the primo throughout the night, losing track of time until my friends eventually bid me farewell. The high felt like freedom. But freedom has a cost. And I had no idea I had just made the most expensive purchase of my life. I thought I was escaping grief. But grief wasn't leaving—it was just getting high with me.

That night seemed perfect, almost too perfect. Unbeknownst to me, I was unwittingly stepping into the clutches of one of the most addictive substances ever known. I deceived myself into believing that I was impervious to addiction, convinced of my own strength. Little did I know, strength had nothing to do with it. The first hit felt like an escape, but in reality I had just taken the first step into a trap that would take years to claw my way out of.

The pain awaiting me would surpass the grief of losing my sister, and the consequences I was about to inflict upon others served as a stark reminder that I was no different from her.

When feeling becomes a threat, you shut it all down. But numbness isn't strength—it's self-abandonment in disguise.

8

LOSS IN LOVE

Navigating through Mirian's funeral was a battle between grief and the overwhelming anger festering inside me. My sister was gone, and I was drowning in a storm of emotions, each one pulling me deeper. My sadness was real, but it was tangled with something darker—a relentless need for vengeance against my brother-in-law Michael. I needed someone to blame. It didn't matter that I lacked proof or that rationality should have stepped in. The grief was too raw, too consuming. My family was in disarray, my mother suffering in a way I couldn't even begin to understand. I could barely manage my own pain, let alone carry hers.

I turned to drinking and smoking weed, hoping for relief that never came. My friends left me a few primos, and they didn't last long. The high was a bandage over a bullet wound—temporary and useless against the real damage underneath. Days passed in a haze. Mirian's death was my first real, gut-wrenching loss. The only other time I had felt anything close was when my grandfather passed two years prior, but that had been expected. His was the kind of death you braced yourself for. No one was prepared to lose Mirian.

My mother told me I didn't have to attend the funeral, trying to ease the weight I was carrying. At the time it felt like an act of mercy, but looking back, I wonder if it only enabled me to avoid confronting my grief head-on. It may not have been the best decision—one made for the moment, not for my long-term healing.

I felt relief at the thought of avoiding the raw finality of it all. But deep down I knew I needed to go. Closure wasn't an option—it was a necessity. Yet something held me back. I imagined the sight of her casket. The physical weight of it in my hands mirrored the emotional weight crushing my body. The unbearable burden wasn't just the casket—it was the knowledge that this was it, the last act of love I could give her. I should be there to bear the final duty of laying her to rest, but I couldn't bring myself to face it. I was afraid of the pain.

My mother worried about my hostility toward Michael, especially with his law enforcement colleagues attending. She was afraid of what I might do, and truthfully, so was I. When the day came, I made the decision that I wouldn't go. It felt like the safest choice at the time, but the moment passed, and guilt settled in. She was gone, and I wouldn't be there to say goodbye.

That morning, reality hit hard. I would never hear her laugh, never get another one of her tight, reassuring hugs. I could barely breathe from the thought of it. I was suffocating. And in that desperation I needed an escape. A primo. But I didn't have one. I had never bought my own before—until that day.

I knew exactly where to go. My feet led me into a neighborhood I had no business being in but was very familiar with. I was seeking out the poison that would dull everything. The dealer barely looked at me as he handed over a twenty-five-dollar rock of cocaine. Just like that, I had taken the first step down a road I never intended to walk. I didn't think about what it meant, what it would lead to. I only knew that for a few hours, maybe even a day, I wouldn't have to feel shit. The first hit was a revelation. The pain, the grief, the guilt—they vanished into the smoke. It was temporary, but in that moment temporary was all I needed.

The days that followed were a whirlwind of emotions I couldn't process—anger, sorrow, regret. I started digging for answers I wasn't prepared for. The details of her death, the gunshot wound, Michael being there. It fueled the fire inside me. I needed to know the truth, but the truth was an abyss I wasn't ready to fall into. Instead, I sought distraction. And in that confusion, in that need for something solid to hold on to, I made an impulsive decision that Melissa and I should move up our wedding date. I proposed we get married right away, driven by the realization that life is too short and that waiting felt like a risk I wasn't willing to take.

I told myself it was because I loved her. And I did. But was it love that made me rush it? Or was it fear? Grief? Or the fear that life can be ripped away without warning? I couldn't answer that then, and maybe a part of me didn't want to. I just knew that I needed something to feel real, to feel stable. Melissa was that for me.

A part of me was racing against the loss, trying to outrun the darkness creeping in. I convinced myself that love was enough to keep me grounded. But love alone couldn't quiet the storm raging inside me. Love couldn't bring Mirian back. And love couldn't erase the fact that the grip of addiction had its hand around my throat.

The weeks that followed were a blur of trying to piece together a life that was rapidly unraveling. I found out Mirian had been struggling more than I ever realized. She had been extremely depressed, possibly even using drugs herself. I didn't want to believe it. I had this image of her—strong, full of life, untouchable. But even the strongest people break. It made me wonder, *Who's looking at me right now, thinking I am strong, while I am falling apart?*

The grief never got easier, but the drugs helped me pretend. I kept pushing forward, pretending I was in control, pretending I was okay. But I wasn't. I had no idea that the worst was yet to come. That this was just the beginning of a battle that would test everything I thought I knew about loss, love, and survival. And that the next time I found myself staring down rock bottom, it wouldn't be from losing someone else. It would be from losing myself.

9

SEEKING DIVERSIONS

After confirming our September wedding date, my fiancée dropped an exhilarating bombshell—the possibility of her being pregnant. Overwhelmed with joy, it felt as though the universe was granting me an opportunity to embrace new life amid the recent sorrow of losing my sister. With marriage on the horizon, the prospect of potential fatherhood, and a growing affection for my soon-to-be stepchildren, life seemed remarkably generous at the age of twenty. Factor in a fulfilling job, a new car, and plans to move into a house, my scene was nothing short of a dream. As we eagerly awaited the doctor's visit, our happiness reached new heights when it was confirmed—she was indeed pregnant, approximately five or six weeks along.

Just one week before our wedding, a sudden and unexpected twist shook my world once again. My fiancée began experiencing severe bleeding, a crisis I felt wholly unprepared to handle. Urged by the doctor, we rushed to the emergency room. After a battery of tests, the heartbreaking news arrived—she had suffered a miscarriage. This would be the first of many to come for us over the years.

The joy we felt turned into profound heartbreak, adding another layer of loss five weeks after my sister's passing. I couldn't help but question the cruelty of such a tragedy, especially when life had seemed so promising. But we persevered, and I doubled down on the grief that already plagued me.

Our wedding came quickly, given the short timeline. I stood at the altar, reciting my vows: "In sickness and in health, until death do us part." The weight of those words should have meant everything, but as I said them, I was already breaking them. I was standing there, sick, addicted, and drowning in a battle I wasn't ready to fight.

We decided on a simple chapel ceremony, attended by both our parents and families. The hotel where I worked surprised us with a suite and a small reception, covering the food and everything. It was a kind gesture, and for a moment it almost felt like the fresh start we needed. Melissa was still recovering from the miscarriage, both physically and emotionally. She was trying to be present, to enjoy the night, but I could see the exhaustion in her eyes. It was a reminder that no matter how much we smiled through the ceremony, the grief was still there, lurking beneath the surface.

And me? I wasn't fully there either. My mind was elsewhere, consumed by a craving I couldn't ignore. Less than six weeks after my first hit, the drug was controlling my mind and body. It was all I could think about. Throughout the evening, I smiled, played my part, and counted the minutes until everyone left. I wasn't thinking about my new wife, my future, or even what the night was supposed to mean. I was just waiting for the moment I could get high.

I couldn't even get through my wedding night without craving a high more than the life I had just committed to. I wasn't starting a new chapter; I was already skipping ahead to the destruction.

What should have been the beginning of a new life was already unraveling. I had convinced myself that I could control it, that I was just taking the edge off. But in that moment, standing in the middle of a hotel suite filled with celebration and love, all I could focus on was feeding the addiction that had already started taking over.

Two months after the wedding, our lives had settled into a routine, but I still yearned for change. I *needed* to escape my inner turmoil. Our apartment felt confining, and Melissa suggested we move to a house, a seemingly perfect solution at the time. The search and planning provided more diversions. Yet I knew I was running from myself, using distractions to evade my demons. Our search led us to a rental home in Carson, twenty miles south of downtown Los Angeles. Three bedrooms, two baths—the perfect setting for our blended family. Amid this transition, I reflected on the past six months—a job promotion, a new car, my sister's death, a miscarriage, marriage, and now, at not even the legal drinking age, playing the role of a family man.

Moving day arrived, and friends lent a hand. A humorous moment unfolded with Tim attempting to carry a refrigerator on his back, providing much-needed laughter among us. Unpacking in our new home, the kids celebrated having their own rooms, and life seemed to move in a positive direction.

I didn't know my newfound tranquility would be short-lived. Those demons I tried to outrun were already ahead of me. The unprocessed pain of losing my sister and the lingering heartache of my wife's miscarriage waged a silent war. These temporary fixes proved inadequate against the deep wounds, and the realization hit hard—the war wasn't against an external enemy but against my own unresolved grief. People will tell you that loss and grief lessen with time. I've always hated this expression, especially while in pain. Grief is like a shadow. It stretches, shrinks, and shifts, but it never really goes away. The hole will always be there, never to be filled again. That pain will remain as strong as it ever was until you find some sense of peace and acceptance, because that unresolved trauma will catch up with you. And distractions will prove futile against those persistent demons.

Little did I know, the worst was yet to come. I was building a life with one hand and burning it down with the other. And my now-wife and stepchildren were oblivious to the monumental changes awaiting them.

10

SHATTERING STEREOTYPES

It was a routine checkout—until she pointed at me. "The Black man stole from me!" The words hit harder than a punch, knocking the damn air out of my lungs. I had worked too hard for this. But this wasn't new. This was another battle in a fight I never asked for.

Amid my initial disbelief, I resolved to excel in my job, driven by a genuine passion for my work. It's crucial to note that I maintained a steadfast commitment to staying clearheaded at work—no substances, no exceptions. Crossing that line was nonnegotiable; my professional reputation meant everything to me. Navigating the hospitality industry as an African American in a predominantly White environment presented its own set of challenges on my journey to success. Prejudice and baseless assumptions often cast a shadow on my professional path, and a specific incident at work served as a stark reminder of the harsh realities of racial biases.

In my role at the hotel, my dedication and professionalism were widely recognized. During a particular check-in, a White woman—an employee from another hotel location—requested a safe-deposit box, and I assisted her accordingly. After securing her items in the box, she joined me in the back office for the process, where I explained the two-key system—one key remaining in the office and the other with her. Two days later, during her checkout with a substantial food and alcohol bill, she made an unfounded claim, accusing "the Black man" of stealing money from her wallet. I felt helpless and frustrated. Here I was, working hard, doing my job, and yet I was right back where I always seemed to be—defending myself against a lie. My job had no idea about my struggles with addiction. They saw me as a dedicated and trustworthy employee, someone who showed up, worked hard, and remained professional. But none of that mattered in this moment—because the only thing they saw was my skin and the accusation.

This false allegation, a blow to my character, triggered a traumatic memory from my childhood, casting a lasting shadow on my life. This wasn't the first time my integrity was questioned simply because of my skin. The last time, I was just a kid. I was thirteen years old when, joyously on my brother-in-law Paul's motorcycle, I was abruptly pulled over by a sheriff's deputy, handcuffed, and taken to an affluent neighborhood to be identified. I was placed in a lineup, and an elderly White man had to discern whether I was the Black kid who'd snatched his wife's purse. He ultimately cleared me. But as I was let go, the officer and the White man's parting words stuck with me: "Good luck, kid." It was said with the sarcastic undertone of "I'll see you again." As if I needed luck to stay out of trouble. Since then I carried an implicit assumption that my life would be marked by hardship because of my skin color—a painful reminder of the stereotypes and prejudices pervading my career.

Back at the hotel, I defended myself against the allegations with dignity, even offering to take a polygraph test to prove my innocence. It was later revealed that the woman had a history of making such accusations, and my character and reputation were eventually restored externally. But internally, the damage was done. There was no official acknowledgment of my innocence. No apology. No real consequence for her false claim. It was brushed under the rug, just like always. I struggled with the embarrassment of this situation.

Despite these adversities and others that followed, my professional journey persisted. As I approached my one-year anniversary at the hotel, I found myself being groomed for the role of a night auditor—an intimidating challenge, requiring the reconciliation of financial records and a shift to a nocturnal routine and reduced guest interaction, but one I was prepared to take on.

Through these trials and tribulations, I learned that courage, determination, and resilience are some of the keys to success. I couldn't stop the world from seeing me through their own biases, but I could refuse to let them define me. This wasn't the first time, and it wouldn't be the last. But I had a choice—let their ignorance break me, or let my resilience write the ending to my own story.

Try this: List three labels or roles you were given growing up. Cross out the ones you've outgrown. Then write a new identity statement that starts with: "I was told I was or wasn't ____, but I know I am ____."

11

VISIBLE SIGNS

Three months into my addiction, and I was already unrecognizable. My reflection in the mirror looked like a man being eaten alive from the inside out—cheeks hollowed, skin dull, eyes carrying secrets I wasn't ready to admit.

Initially, my use was sporadic, but over time the craving to get high became all-encompassing, seizing me at every opportunity. Compounding this destructive cycle was my financial struggle; earning only $6.50 per hour, I found myself squandering money at an alarming rate. My biweekly paychecks, which hit every other Thursday, were instantly swallowed by my addiction, leaving me in disbelief as I started referring to myself as a "crackhead"—a label I promptly dismissed. Surely, I rationalized I couldn't be that far gone, right? Yet by Saturday, my paychecks all but vanished in the smoke of a two-day binge, forcing me to confront the harsh reality.

My wife was my first major casualty of this destructive cycle. She witnessed helplessly as the man she married spiraled further out of control. I reassured her with empty promises, pretending to have a grip on my situation, but the truth was evident in our dwindling savings, unpaid bills, and overdue rent. Her shared, rampant concerns washed over me—heard but never truly absorbed. As weeks blurred into months, my condition continued to spiral downward, and I continued to squander our income on drugs. I maintained a facade of control, whispering hollow assurances to myself that I could quit whenever I wished. But my internal nagging persisted: *Can I quit, really?*

Half a year into my descent, the physical manifestations of my addiction had become impossible to ignore. Layers of clothing concealed a twenty-pound weight loss, but there was no hiding a big head and my sunken cheeks. My clothes hung on me like a dead man's suit. My reflection, a ghost. My wife's eyes, a mix of sadness and anger, like she was staring at the man she loved trapped inside a stranger's body.

Friends and family began to notice. Questions about my health, startling weight loss, and the darkness in my eyes poured in, but I deflected with half-ass excuses. I attributed it all to work stress and the loss of Mirian. I used her tragic passing as a scapegoat for my decisions. It was a painful rationalization. On the outside I still maintained the facade of a functioning adult, attending work diligently. No one knew I was constantly wrestling with the overwhelming urge to get high. I refused to acknowledge the possibility of having a problem, let alone being addicted. The only addiction I ever envisioned was a vivacious sex life, not this self-destructive path. But with each passing day, the relentless urges intensified, challenging my claim of internal strength. The reality was sobering: Crack cocaine had fucked me up.

Facing my daily work routine became an enormous challenge. The drain of addiction and the ever-present temptation at my workplace became near insurmountable hurdles. As a front desk clerk in a bustling hotel, handling a cash drawer was part of my responsibility. Every shift felt like a countdown to disaster. My hands trembled every time I counted the cash drawer, and my heart raced every time a coworker looked at me too long. One wrong move and it was over. I'd be labeled. Fired. Exposed. And yet the craving didn't care about consequences—it just wanted to be fed. The threat to my reputation, the trust I'd built, and the respect I'd earned were at stake. I was the first Black employee to hold this position in the hotel's history, and the weight of paving the way for others was never far from my thoughts. Every day was a grueling battle between preserving my job and quitting. This job was the final lifeline to my self-esteem and financial stability. Was I going to succumb to the relentless pressures of my addiction and jeopardize my professional career? The question I needed to ask myself wasn't *if*, but *when*.

My wife suggested rehab as a possible solution, but I quickly dismissed the idea, associating it with surrender. Despite the undeniable signs—the weight loss, the cravings, and the looming danger of my secret unraveling at work—I maintained that I was still in control. The reality was that I was out of control. My identity was beginning to fade away, and for the first time, I felt powerless and helpless to this drug. After much deliberation, and against a backdrop of growing fear and anxiety, I finally agreed to seek help. The decision did bring a small sense of relief but also a crippling dread. Admitting that I was going to rehab felt like a public admission of failure. The illusion of the invincible Jonathan, who never let anything take control, was cracking. We explored options and settled on a reputable facility in Pasadena, California, one that caters to celebrities and the affluent. The irony of a young Black man from a humble background entering such an upscale place because of insurance coverage added an unsettling layer to the situation. There were no more excuses left for me to hide behind.

The looming question of how to request a leave of absence from work without revealing the real reason was terrifying. I finally mustered the courage to tell my manager that I needed time off because of family issues, only to be met with her regretful response: the only option was to quit. I was stunned into silence, and after a deep breath, I heard myself saying the unthinkable: "Well then, I must quit." My response shocked her in turn, and she headed off to initiate my resignation process. After a brief discussion with the general manager, she returned with unexpected news. I was granted the thirty-day leave of absence I'd requested. The relief was palpable, yet beneath it I felt the gears shifting toward my unknown journey.

Securing my leave was only the first step. The following days were a blur of preparation and quiet reflection, a deceptive calm before the inevitable storm. As I shared my plans with my wife, the look of simultaneous relief and worry on her face mirrored my own feelings. Was this the turning point or just another false start in a long string of failed attempts? I wanted to believe this time would be different, but doubt had a way of creeping in when I least expected it.

The thought of walking into rehab was frightening. It was a world I knew nothing about yet one I had fought so hard to avoid. I imagined the cold sterility of the place, chaos, and noisy halls filled with people whose lives had unraveled just like mine. I wasn't like them, I told myself. But then again I wasn't sure who I was anymore. Would I feel out of place? Would I be judged? Or, worse, would I finally have to face the truth I had spent so long running from? I was a damn addict. The real battle wasn't ahead of me. It was inside me. And it had already begun.

Not all damage shows up in bruises. Sometimes the most visible signs of trauma are the ones you normalize.

PART II

RECKONING—BREAK WHAT'S BEEN BREAKING YOU

You can't heal what you still defend.

12

REHAB NO. 1: THE DENIAL

The car ride felt like a slow march to execution. Every mile, every traffic light was a countdown to a reality I wasn't ready to face. I wasn't an addict, at least that was what I told myself. But if that were true, why was I sitting in this car, heading to rehab, hands clenched into fists, my stomach tight with dread?

Upon checking into rehab, my initial instinct was to isolate myself. But the staff had other ideas and insisted on integrating me—touring the facility, shaking hands, and looking into the eyes of people I swore I had nothing in common with. Silently I pleaded to be left alone, away from the presence of addicts. In my mind I wasn't one of them. I was different. I was better. But deep down a voice I wasn't ready to hear whispered, "Then why the hell are you here?"

After a couple of days, my guard began to lower. I started interacting with others, attending group sessions, and surprisingly, anticipating the substantial meals and snacks meant to help me regain lost weight. The narratives shared during group sessions were eye-opening, filled with stories of profound loss—jobs, cars, homes, families, and self-respect. Some were fresh out of jail, with rehab being part of their sentence. Despite their struggles, I maintained a self-assured stance, insisting that I was not like them. I had no tragic stories of my own to share.

After five days, I was ready to get high. It was the first time in six months I had gone this many days without using, and the itch under my skin felt unbearable. I could feel the craving creeping back, whispering to me, convincing me that I had done enough, that I had proven I could stop if I wanted to. But I hadn't proven anything yet.

By the seventh day, I sought excuses to leave. Convinced I didn't share the same damn problems as my fellow patients, I battled intense urges and withdrawals. The cravings grew stronger, and I convinced myself it was time to abandon rehab.

In a desperate attempt to escape, I fabricated a story about a job opportunity in Hawaii that required me to leave the next day. I was spreading the lie around the facility. However, during a group session later that day, my counselor exposed the lie in front of everyone. He said, "Hey, everyone, guess what? Jonathan is lying to us. I called his wife, and she knows nothing about this story." Oh shit, I was busted. Game recognized game. The humiliation. The embarrassment. I was overwhelmed, and in a twisted attempt at justification, I lashed out, proclaiming, "Fuck you! Fuck all of you!" I still saw myself as the victim. They were wrong, not me. I shouted out yet again, "Fuck you! I'm leaving!" The counselor stopped me for a few minutes, warning me about the consequences of leaving. He looked me dead in the eyes and said, "If you leave, you'll be back. It may not be here, but it will be somewhere. And you will be telling the same stories as everyone else." His words carried the weight of a truth I wasn't ready to accept, emphasizing the cycle of rehab, jail, or death that awaited me if I didn't change. In my emotional state, I couldn't comprehend the unseen repercussions. Angered, I called my wife, cursing her out, "What the fuck did you tell them?" and demanding she pick me up. Despite her confusion, I dismissed her questions, rushed to pack my belongings, and left the hospital, ignoring pleas from fellow patients.

Sitting on the curb, waiting for my wife, I hid behind parked cars, evading the counselor and patients searching for me. This person, who believed they had no addiction, was now overwhelmed by embarrassment and fear because of their own deception. My wife finally arrived, and as we drove home, I felt a sinking realization that I would likely be high again soon. The challenge to stay clean and resist falling back into my dysfunctional life had just begun. The drive home felt long with a whirlwind of thoughts in my head.

As I stepped inside my supposed sanctuary, my house felt tainted, and the real struggle to stay clean commenced. I faced the daunting challenge of proving to myself that I could overcome addiction without spiraling down again, navigating an uncertain path with no clear answers about who I would become. Returning home intensified my cravings as withdrawal set in. In my mind playing the victim became an excuse to justify getting high, but for the first time, guilt crept in. Despite learning a few coping mechanisms during my short stint in rehab, the resources to stop this seemed insufficient.

Ten days without drugs ended when I found myself at the dope house, spiraling back into the cycle. As my addiction worsened over the next several months, I became fixated on getting high, depleting paychecks within hours and accumulating unpaid bills.

Despite my job's significance and the sense of structure it provided, the temptation to use was suffocating. Each day I walked into that building, I was walking into a battle, and the cracks in my armor were growing wider. The stress of simply being there, pretending everything was fine while my mind was at war with itself, was unbearable.

Paranoia that my colleagues knew—knew I was an addict, knew I was slipping, knew I was one mistake away from losing the fragile reputation I had built—slithered into my thoughts like a silent intruder. Every side glance, every hushed conversation, every casual question about how I was doing felt like an interrogation. Were they testing me? Did they see the twenty pounds of weight loss? Did they notice the exhaustion on my face, the jitteriness in my hands? My anxiety turned routine interactions into psychological warfare.

I told myself that I could maintain control. That I could separate my professional self from my addict self. That I could clock out and go back to the madness without it bleeding into my work life. But that was a lie. I spent every minute in that job waiting for the other shoe to drop, waiting for someone to ask the wrong question, waiting for my performance to slip just enough for them to start putting the pieces together.

Then came the breaking point. The moment when the weight of my double life became too much. I would either break or be exposed, and I wasn't willing to let that happen. My reputation, whatever was left of it, had to be preserved. And so I quit. Abruptly. No warning. No plan. Just the desperate need to get out before my facade crumbled.

At first the relief was immense. No more pressure, no more pretending. But that feeling was short-lived. The reality of my decision hit me like a freight train. With no job, no money, and no eligibility for unemployment, the stability I had managed to hold on to, however shaky, was now gone. I fell hard, and there was no safety net waiting to catch me.

Melissa, who had fought so hard to keep our household together despite my chaos, was now bearing the full weight of my self-destruction. The worry in her eyes, the stress lining her face—it was all because of me. The toll it took on her health was unmistakable. The stress ate away at her. She barely slept. Her movements were slower, her energy drained. The life we had built, the one I had sworn to protect, was now crumbling under the weight of my choices.

And my step-kids—they weren't just collateral damage; they were also casualties in a war they never signed up for. The man who had once promised them stability and love had become a ghost, haunting the house with his absence. They felt it, even if they didn't fully understand it. The disappointment in my stepson's eyes, the confusion on my stepdaughter's face—those moments stung more than any withdrawal ever could.

Yet in the midst of all this, my mind had room for only one thing: my next high. It didn't matter that my world was burning around me. It didn't matter that the people I loved were drowning in the mess I had created. The only thing that mattered was escaping the crushing reality of it all. And so I chased the very thing that was destroying me.

There was no plan. No strategy. No sense of direction. Just the relentless, insatiable hunger for another hit. And as I spiraled deeper, I didn't just lose my job—I also lost self-respect and the last remaining shred of control I had over my life.

13

THE REAL PROBLEM

Crack cocaine, an exceptionally potent and addictive substance, presents a formidable challenge to quit. However, the difficulty doesn't solely stem from its potency. The withdrawal symptoms far surpass the fear of addiction itself. The onset of withdrawal effects varies but typically begins within hours to a few days after discontinuation, extending for up to twenty-eight weeks. Yes, that's right—up to seven months of symptoms, ranging from depression, irritability, extreme fatigue, increased appetite, increased need for sleep, vivid and unpleasant dreams to anxiety, severe drug cravings, and even psychosis. The intensity and severity of these symptoms can fluctuate based on various factors, such as the extent of your addiction, duration of use, quantity and frequency, and whether you are concurrently using other substances with crack cocaine, including alcohol.

In addition to the abovementioned withdrawal effects, you might experience post-acute withdrawal symptoms that extend well beyond the cessation of usage, particularly with a history of heavy abuse. Some of these symptoms may persist for weeks after your last use. Signs of post-acute withdrawal from crack cocaine might involve difficulties with short-term memory, mood fluctuations, disruptions in sleep, episodes of panic attacks, and an inability to experience pleasure, commonly referred to as anhedonia.

Crack cocaine withdrawal happens in three stages. First is the crash. Most users go through a crash within a few hours to a few days after discontinuing crack use. Symptoms in this stage encompass heightened appetite, exhaustion, irritability, a heightened need for sleep, and restlessness. Second is withdrawal. Following the subsidence (the sinking feeling) of the initial crash, the second phase of withdrawal may span up to ten weeks. During this stage you might encounter crack cocaine withdrawal effects, including heightened cravings, irritability, sleepiness, and difficulties with concentration. The third and final stage is extinction. Former users may undergo intermittent cravings, often influenced by social situations and triggers, such as associations with individuals with whom crack cocaine was previously used or being in environments where the substance is available.*

THE REAL FEAR OF EVERY ADDICT: THE STRUGGLE OF WITHDRAWAL

Therein lies the real fear of every addict: withdrawal. I know that's a general statement, but I'd wager it's almost wholly accurate. It's not just the physical agony—though that alone is enough to break most people. The real terror lies in what withdrawal forces you to face. The moment the high is gone, all that's left is you—raw, exposed, and drowning in the very things you tried to escape.

*Dan Wagener, "Crack Cocaine Withdrawal Symptoms and Stages," American Addiction Centers, updated August 28, 2024, withdrawal.net/cocaine/crack-symptoms-effects-stages.

I learned this the hard way. My first stint in rehab scared the hell out of me. The symptoms hit fast—the shakes, the nausea, the restlessness that made my skin crawl—but none of that compared to the silence. In the stillness I wasn't just battling cravings. I was also battling every buried memory, every untold story, every scar I had refused to acknowledge. I thought I was going to rehab to quit drugs. What I didn't realize was that I was also about to meet every ghost from my past—Mirian's suicide, the loss of my first child, the father who wasn't there, the mother who couldn't see me, and the six-year-old boy inside me who had been carrying a secret for too long. I wasn't ready for that.

I walked into rehab thinking I had a drug problem. I walked out realizing drugs weren't the problem at all. They were just the symptom. The real disease was the grief I refused to feel, the self-worth I never built, and the fear that if I let go of my pain, I'd have nothing left.

I did what most addicts do when they aren't ready: I ran. *I chose the devil I knew over the unknown I feared.* I wasn't willing to sit in that kind of pain, to let withdrawal rip me apart and leave me with nothing but my own reflection. So I did what felt natural: I left, convinced myself I wasn't "that bad," and ran right back into the arms of my addiction. But here's the thing about running: You eventually run out of places to go.

If you feel this applies to you, make a list of your top three coping mechanisms. This could be food, work, social media, sex, weed, alcohol, staying busy, isolating, etc. Now ask: What pain are they covering? Name the root, not the behavior.

14

ANOTHER BROKEN HOME

After I quit my job, my addiction became my life. My hours were dedicated to hustling any way I could—pawning, scamming, making deals—just to keep the high going, to quiet the noise in my head and escape the weight of everything crushing me. Occasionally, I would manage a brief respite—just three precious days without succumbing to the grip of drugs. Yet when withdrawal crept in, any semblance of that control dissolved. Consecutive nights were lost in the fog of addiction. How many? I can't be sure.

At some point my wife asked me if my sister Candace, her husband, and their two children could stay with us for a while. Bewildered, I asked why. She explained they were facing eviction with nowhere to go, and Candace reached out for help. As her words lingered in the air, I grappled with my own turmoil and the surrounding darkness that situation would cause. The last thing I needed was more people in this house, especially considering my sister's quick temper and pregnancy. Despite my reservations, I reluctantly agreed, almost as if Candace were my wife's sister, not mine. To accommodate this change, we rearranged, squeezing our two kids into one bedroom.

In the weeks that followed, I found myself retreating more and more, as if searching for a reason to escape. Looking back, I'm sure I was. Candace and I were not close. Not like Mirian and me. Having her there was an ever-present reminder that Mirian wasn't. And after just a few weeks, our rocky relationship came to a head. My wife and brother-in-law Chris had just run out to the grocery store, and Candace was in an especially bad mood. My stepdaughter was playing with my niece, and with no real reason, other than her foul mood, my sister banished them to the bedroom. My stepdaughter, frustrated and on the verge of tears, blurted out, "I'm tired of her always telling me to go to my room!" And rightfully so. This wasn't the first time they were barred from the living room. As I walked in the room, I caught Candace heatedly chastising my stepdaughter. A fierce protectiveness came over me, and I intervened, urging my sister to back down. "In this house, we don't banish anyone. You are a guest, and this is our house." Candace, ill-tempered person that she was, lost it, telling me she was going to bring this matter to my wife. Infuriated, I asserted my authority, declaring that I was handling it, and that's the end of it.

In a fit of rage, my sister delivered the devastating blow. She looked me dead in the eye and spat, "You are the reason Mirian killed herself. You knew everything going on, and you did nothing. And everyone knows it." For a moment the room fell silent, as if even the walls recoiled from her words. My breath caught in my throat. It felt like my stomach had caved in, like something inside me had cracked open. I was standing when she said it. My whole body tensed, blood rushed to my head, and I gripped the back of the couch to steady myself, but nothing could ground me. The weight of guilt I had fought so hard to suppress threatened to crush me. My legs wobbled beneath me, and before I could stop them, tears streamed down my face. "What did you say?" She repeated it, her voice colder this time, "You are the reason Mirian killed herself. You knew everything going on and did nothing. And everyone knows it." Then she smirked. I was so fucking angry. My fists clenched at my sides. My whole body burned with rage. "You bitch," I snapped. "You evil bitch."

She wielded those words like daggers, aiming to wound, and she succeeded. "Get the fuck out of my house!" My voice shook. "Now!"

I didn't care if she and her family had nowhere to go. But she remained defiant, arguing that my wife invited her, and it wasn't my place to "throw her out onto the streets." She provoked me further, daring me to strike her so she could call the police. I had to catch myself. My hands balled into fists, and my entire body coiled with rage. Every part of me wanted to swing, to make her feel even a fraction of the pain she had just inflicted. But I forced myself to stop, breathing hard, my nails digging into my palms. I resisted, mindful of her unborn child. So I started tossing their belongings into the driveway. It was all I could do as the tears continued to run down my cheeks. In an unexpected moment, my five-year-old niece approached, saying, "Uncle John, Uncle John, Uncle John, I love you." In that moment I froze, overcome with sadness and tears.

My wife and brother-in-law came home to a chaotic scene—clothes, toiletries, and the baby bed scattered across the lawn. My wife sensed the gravity of the situation and rushed toward me, confused and questioning. I could barely breathe. Through tearful sobs and a snotty nose, I repeated my sister's accusation. My wife was shocked. She was well aware of the deep cut Candace's words had left and agreed that they had to leave. She asked if she could give them a few days to get their stuff together—a testament to her unwavering kindness. So they lingered for three more agonizing days—among the longest of my life. I barely spoke. I barely slept. Every time I heard her voice, my chest tightened. The house felt like a pressure cooker—one wrong move and everything would explode. Candace acted like nothing had happened, but I could feel her words circling me, waiting to strike again.

Endless questions tormented me—Who believes this accusation? Was it whispered behind my back? What do they know that I don't?

Candace moved out and on from that day like it had never happened. We didn't speak for about a year. Despite the turmoil she knowingly caused, she never offered an explanation or an apology for her words.

The wound from that accusation festered within me and spread like cancer. My addiction tightened its hold that day. Every day thereafter was a dance with disaster. The stress weighed heavily on my marriage, and the financial strain made it impossible to dig ourselves out of the hole we were in. With every hit, every rush, I was pulled further away from the chance of a normal, peaceful life. Despite the countless moments that showed me I needed to stop, the pull of the drugs kept dragging me back. The irony of it all was that the very thing I turned to for escape was the catalyst for the chaos in my life. And I still lit up.

15

NO EXIT

There's no way out when the prison is your own mind. Motel rooms weren't just graveyards. They were also morgues for the living—places where men like me decomposed in real time, one hit at a time. I never checked into these rooms; I surrendered to them. No baggage, no ID. If walls could talk, these wouldn't bother. Rooms were rented by the hour, the comforters a crime scene of stains, each one telling a story I didn't want to know. The air was thick with cigarettes, sweat, and desperation. Moans from the next room. A slap. A scream. Prostitutes arguing in the hallway. A deal gone bad.

These weren't places you stayed. These were places you hid. *But hiding doesn't erase who you are. It just delays the moment you have to face it.*

At five, six, and seven years old, the bathroom had been my sanctuary. I would isolate myself there, sometimes for twenty to thirty minutes at a time. *The ways we teach ourselves to survive as children don't always let us live as adults.* My isolation wasn't new; it was just more refined, more permanent. I thought I was just hiding as a kid. I never realized I was rehearsing for a lifetime of disappearing.

The more time I spent in solitude, the more these old fears, these raw feelings began to resurface. *Trauma waits. It doesn't knock. It doesn't announce itself. It just sits in the dark, waiting for you to be alone.*

Paranoia was always waiting for me. It didn't end when I found a place to hide; it just changed shape. The cocaine had my eyes stretched wide open, my heart slamming against my ribs at every sound. A shadow moving too fast. A gust of wind blowing trash. A car door slamming.

In the motel room, the paranoia mutated. Instead of watching my surroundings, I watched the door. The phone. The window. I'd sit in the dark, pressing two fingers against the edge of the curtain, peeking through the gap like a desperate fugitive. Every shadow outside meant something. Every voice in the hallway was a threat. Again and again, I checked. I wasn't sure who I was running from, *me or a stranger.*

Leaving was always the hardest part. When my hours were up, I had to stumble back into reality, high, needing more, but forced to face whatever version of myself could fake it for a few hours. On the way home, I'd sit in my car watching the city move like it belonged to people who had their shit together. But I wasn't part of that world anymore. I belonged to the shadows. The forgotten corners. The empty parking lots in the industrial areas, where no one asked questions, and no one cared. No cops, no witnesses, just me and my high. But in the silence, something else lurked. Something I couldn't outrun. And then he showed up . . . Little John-John.

At first, he was just a whisper. Then a presence. Then a fight. I didn't know what trauma was, not really. But John-John did. And he wanted me to feel it. He had questions. I didn't have answers. He had pain. I didn't want to feel it. He had memories. I had spent my entire life trying to bury them. Then like a bullet to the brain, the question hit me.

Was I molested?

It was so sudden, so violent, that I said it out loud. "No fucking way. It can't be." But the memories were coming, and I couldn't stop them. *Nah. Not me. I'd remember if it happened, right? This shit only happens to other people. Not to me. Not to me.*

One voice inside me screamed, "Shut the fuck up, little boy!" The other whimpered, "Let me be free." And then I saw him. The little boy I used to be. The boy I had abandoned. If I had a gun that night, it would have been a double homicide—the kid and me—because the pain was too great, too vast, and too unbearable for both of us.

My body burned from my soul like an unbreakable fever. My mind spiraled. And then my inner child, sad and scared, finally spoke up. "I was molested. And I'm sorry. I was only six, and I didn't know better."

The past, buried under years of secrecy, had finally broken through. The combination of drugs and isolation brought more detailed memories to the surface, hitting me as if it had just happened. And suddenly I existed in three versions of myself at once: A drug addict in a motel room, drowning in cocaine and regret. A six-year-old child, small and scared, standing in the shadow of a predator, with no one to protect him. And a twenty-one-year-old man, carrying fifteen years of pain, unable to carry the weight that little John-John had carried all these years. I felt cowardly not protecting him.

In the past he lacked the ability to articulate it, as the act itself was a silent ordeal. It wasn't something we spoke about back in the day. I had been taught not to let anyone touch my private parts as a child and to confide in someone if it occurred. But no one told me it was bad. No one taught me how to tell when an adult was manipulating my six-year-old mind.

However, the little boy within me swore never to speak of it once he recognized it for what it was. And then the weight of responsibility crushed me. I *held myself accountable* for the abuse I endured.

As a child, I lived next to my abuser, the adult son of our landlord. He was a *known pedophile.* Everyone in my neighborhood, including my own family, was aware of his problematic behavior, but nobody anticipated that I would become his victim. Now, as I grappled with my drug addiction, the guilt I'd suppressed for years intensified. The only thing I could do was continue using.

Deep down I felt it was my duty to *protect this little boy.* But he and I were one and the same. My silence denied me the opportunity to have someone defend me, to reassure me that what happened wasn't my fault. And that secrecy slowly *eroded my childhood innocence.*

As the weeks passed, Melissa kept asking, "What's wrong?" She knew something was off. She hadn't seen me this withdrawn since the day of my sister's death. After weeks, the burden was too much to carry. But the thought of revealing my past to anyone terrified me. My drug use increased, but nothing worked. I couldn't numb this pain like I was able to numb the loss of Mirian.

But who could I trust to confide in? Melissa was the first to come to mind. I didn't know if I could look her in the eye. She had been through so much already. Why place this additional burden on her? I was beginning to use her feelings as my reason to justify not telling her. Eventually I mustered the courage to tell her, with tears rolling down my face. Her response was nothing short of compassionate.

She put her arms around me, pulled me in, and said, "It's okay, Jonathan. It's okay. This was not your fault. You were just a little boy, and I am sorry this happened to you. I am honored you trusted me enough to tell me. I know this was a hard thing for you to do." Her compassionate response offered me the validation and understanding I'd longed for. The most powerful part? I was still standing. Her words *saved me*. But my mother's did not.

That initial validation from Melissa gave me strength to share with my mom. "Why didn't you say something years ago?" she asked. And then the dagger to my chest: "Are you gay or something?" As if this was a coming out.

Her voice wasn't soft or motherly. It was an accusation. A defense mechanism. A slap in the face when I was already bleeding out. And in that moment she confirmed my greatest fear. What would people think? If my own mother felt this way, what would everyone else think? My father? My homies? My brothers? I had finally spoken my truth, and instead of comfort, I was met with exactly what I had feared most: doubt, shame, and judgment. In that moment I was six-year-old John-John again—lost, vulnerable, desperate, and crying.

The pain of my sister's death had been unbearable. But this? This was a hundred times worse. Because this wasn't just grief. This was my own death while still being alive. To feel it. To see it. To touch it. And with it, the addiction that ignited after Mirian's suicide didn't just persist; it escalated, consuming me on an entirely new level.

Every time I thought I'd hit rock bottom, I realized there was still further to fall. I told myself I could stop anytime. That I was still the one in control. But control is the first casualty of addiction; it slips through your fingers before you even realize you've lost it.

Try this: Forget hope. Forget strength. Just finish this sentence without censoring yourself: "If one more thing breaks, I..."

This isn't about collapsing. It's about telling the truth before you do.

16

DISMANTLING THE HOUSE

Two years deep. Two years of chasing the same high, telling myself I still had control. I didn't. And yet here I was—same streets, same routine, same lie. I rolled up to the dealer, my pulse steady, my face unreadable. I forced confidence, the kind that came from doing this too many times but still hating myself for it.

"Let me get a ten-dollar bag of weed and a twenty-dollar rock." No pleasantries. No small talk. Just business. The dealer barely looked at me as he passed off the two small bags. I took them and peeled off in fear of the police, the weight of my reality pressing down on me harder than ever.

I drove a few blocks before pulling over, hands tight on the wheel. I tore open the weed bag first. Dry. Brittle. Lifeless. Not the usual dark green. Not the strong skunky scent. Just some crumbled-up garbage that looked like it had been pulled from a field of weeds.

I swallowed hard. Maybe it was fine. Maybe I was just paranoid. But I knew better. My stomach clenched. My pulse ticked faster. Something told me I was about to be mad as hell. I turned to the most important bag, tore it open, and stared. A rock. A real, solid, smooth-ass, useless rock. I blinked. Once. Twice. I pulled the pebble out, rolling it between my fingers. A lump formed in my throat. My body stiffened as frustration crawled under my skin, hot and sharp. I placed it back in the bag, slid it under my tire, reversed, and checked it again. Still a rock. Not even a damn chip.

I let out a hollow laugh, half amusement, half pure despair. *Even the streets were scamming me now.* I sat there, hands locked on the steering wheel, my veins pulsing like live wires. Anger and disbelief. Did I just get fucked? I already knew the answer. The irony was so thick it almost choked me. If this wasn't my life in one perfect metaphor, I didn't know what was.

THE HUSTLE

How do I get money for my next high? That was my full-time job. Forget career ambitions. Forget relationships. Forget even basic human decency. Nothing else mattered. If you saw me, you wouldn't recognize me. I was down forty pounds, a walking skeleton in baggy clothes, barely clinging to the illusion of the person I used to be.

Cheekbones like blades. Eyes sunken deep. Arms that looked borrowed from someone else. I tried to hide it. Two pairs of pants. Extra layers. As if fooling the mirror would somehow fix the rest of my life. Every day I hit the streets, begging for money with fabricated stories—gas, food, car trouble. Every day a new excuse. Every stranger a new mark. Some looked at me with pity. Others with disgust. Some handed me a dollar—a dollar that wouldn't save me but would get me just a little closer to oblivion.

My addiction had reached a dangerous level. I had no trust in myself. No self-control. Every moment was dictated by the next fix. And I was powerless. I was dragging my wife and step-kids through hell. The love in my house? Replaced with tension. With fear. With exhaustion. I could feel the shift; the warmth was gone. Conversations were shorter. Laughter was rare. They were holding on but just barely.

THE GOODBYE I BEGGED FOR

The day I told my wife to leave was the day I lost my soul. I had just come down from an all-night binge, my body drained, my mind barely holding on. And I knew. I knew it was over.

I didn't just tell her to leave. I begged—dropped to my knees, nose running, tears pouring, voice cracking under the weight of my own destruction. "Take the kids and go. Save them. Save yourself. Please go." I wasn't saying it out of love. I was saying it out of fear. I was scared for them. I couldn't let them stay and watch me self-destruct. I couldn't let them see me hit rock bottom in real time, right in front of their eyes. They deserved a chance at a normal life. And I knew I couldn't be the reason they didn't get it.

Why didn't I leave? Because I had nowhere to go. No money. No job. And eviction was already breathing down my neck. The best thing for Melissa and the kids was to be free of me. She knew it. I knew it. "I hope you find your way back," she said.

Then she was gone. No yelling. No arguing. Just gone. That was how broken she was. And that was how lost I was. It was one of the saddest days of my life. I wasn't choosing drugs over my family anymore. Drugs had already made the choice for me.

THE WRECKAGE

As the day faded into night, I found myself alone, standing in the middle of what used to be a home. Now it was just wreckage. No warmth. No life. No family. No lifeline. No money. No food. And no drugs. Just silence. Just the sound of my own breathing. Just the weight of what I had become.

The silence didn't last long because almost immediately my mind locked onto one thing—my next high. Nothing else mattered. Not the empty house. Not my empty life. Just the next hit.

One might think I couldn't sink any lower. But I did. Over the next two months, I dismantled the house piece by piece and sold everything—furniture, TVs, beds, tools. Anything that could bring in money for another hit was fair game.

If I could have ripped the house off its foundation, I would've made the news—*blocking the freeway with a damn house.* Traffic backed up for miles. News helicopters circling. Reporters losing their minds. "Breaking news: Some idiot just put a three-bedroom, two-bath house in the fast lane." And where was I headed? The pawnshop. Rolling up like, "Hey, man, how much can I get for this?"

TOILET MONEY

I started eyeing the house itself. Desperate, I grabbed a thick Yellow Pages phone book, flipping through it like it held the secret to salvation. I wasn't looking for a job. I was looking for something to sell. Page after page. Nothing. Restaurants. Roofing. Real estate. Useless. Over an hour in, I was still flipping, my fingers smudged with ink, my patience hanging by a thread.

One thousand pages of businesses I had no business with. And then finally—plumbing. My eyes locked onto an ad: "We Buy Used Plumbing Fixtures! TOP DOLLAR PAID!" I stared at it. And then my junkie brain whispered an idea. *You've got a house with two bathrooms, right?*

I couldn't haul a bathtub. But a toilet? That I could work with. I grabbed the phone, my body twitching with impatience. I needed this call to go right. I needed a yes. I lifted the receiver, my fingers pressing hard against the buttons like I could make the answer come faster.

My voice was steady. My body wasn't. I was itching for a fix, my pulse thumping in my ears as I forced myself to sound casual. "How much for a used toilet?" I asked, as if this was the most normal conversation in the world. The guy on the other end didn't even pause. "Depends on the condition," he said, like people sold him toilets every day. "Up to a hundred bucks." That was all I needed to hear. I had a toilet to sell.

I had never removed a toilet before, but *nothing teaches a man new skills like desperation.* After prying and yanking, the damn thing finally gave, still attached to chunks of tile, scraping against the floor as I dragged it through the house like a dead body.

My car, an old, busted Datsun, was barely big enough for me, let alone a toilet. I wedged it into the hatchback, tied it down with a scrap of electrical wire, and prayed it wouldn't fly out on the freeway. My gas tank was on fumes, so this was a one-way trip if the buyer said no. I'd be stranded with a big-ass toilet.

After a forty-five-minute drive, I pulled up, the toilet rattling in the back like it was having second thoughts. I dragged it out, setting it down like a precious artifact in front of the buyer. He didn't say a word at first. Just looked at me. Then at the toilet. Then back at me. It was a look I had seen too many times, the kind that silently asks, "How the hell did your life get to this point?" Finally, he sighed. "Fifty bucks." I pushed back. "Fifty-five." I needed gas. Maybe a little food. And of course, the rest for drugs. He nodded, and the deal was done.

By midnight the drugs were gone, and I was left crashing into loneliness, drowning in depression, staring down the only thing I had left—the impending reality of homelessness.

SHE STOPPED FIGHTING

Occasionally, my wife would drop by the house to pick up extra clothes and check on me. One of those visits still haunts me. She walked in and froze. The house was unrecognizable. The walls were bare. The floors were scattered with discarded clothes and broken remnants of our life. Then her eyes landed on the hole in the bathroom floor. That was when she knew. She turned to look at me, and I saw it all. Shock. Grief. Horror. For the first time, I saw something else in her face: fear. Because she knew I was entering the most dangerous stage of my addiction. And I wasn't coming back.

Then came the day that stopped everything. I walked into the living room and froze. She was standing there. Silent. Shaking. A butcher knife pressed against her wrist. My breath caught, my chest tightening so hard it felt like my ribs might crack. I couldn't move. I couldn't speak. All I could do was stand there, paralyzed, my mind screaming, *No! No! No!* I begged—silently, desperately—for this moment not to turn into something I could never undo. Every terrible thing I had done. Every lie. Every broken promise. Every moment I had neglected her, abandoned her, and made her feel invisible.

It had all led to this. I stepped forward, my hands trembling, my voice barely above a whisper. "Please." I tried to comfort her, to fix what I had shattered. I swore I would change. I promised I would undo the damage, rewind time, and make it right. But how do you pull someone back from a ledge when you're already dangling off it yourself?

MY LIFE, HIS SHOES

In that moment the horrifying truth slammed into me. I wasn't just witnessing a crisis. I was the crisis. I was mirroring Mirian's exact nightmare. The one I accused her husband of creating. The man I had despised. I had spent years condemning him, blaming him for pushing my sister to a place so dark, so hopeless that she thought she had no way out. I never imagined I'd be that kind of man. And yet here I was, standing in his place, watching history repeat itself in real time, except this time I was the one pulling someone else to the edge.

I wasn't just living through my sister's pain. I was the cause of it. I had become the very man I swore I never would. The thought of having to face her family, to look them in the eyes and admit that I was the man who broke her the way I had once damned my brother-in-law, made me feel like I could vomit. But there was no time to process it. No time to feel the shame, the regret, and the disgust at what I had become. Because in that moment, my wife was breaking right in front of me. And my kids, they were losing their mother in real time.

I wasn't just destroying myself. I was also infecting everyone around me. The pain I had inflicted wasn't just hers to bear. It was bleeding into every person connected to us. This wasn't just my downfall. It was a chain reaction of suffering. One hit after another, spreading like wildfire, consuming everything in its path. My wife. My step-kids. My in-laws. No one was spared. Every single one of them was caught in the fallout of my addiction, forced to live in the wreckage I had created. And the damage? *It wasn't just emotional. It was generational.*

After what felt like an eternity but was only ten, maybe fifteen minutes, I finally got the knife from her hand. She didn't fight me. She just collapsed into me, sobbing, screaming, unraveling in my arms.

But the nightmare wasn't over. Before I could even process what had just happened, she broke free. She lunged for the phone, yanked the cord, and before I could react, wrapped it around her neck. Her eyes—wild, frantic, empty. This wasn't just pain. This was a person who had lost all hope. Panic slammed into me. I grabbed at the cord, my mind racing, but she fought me. She wasn't letting go. And for the first time, I wasn't sure if I could save her. I ripped the cord away, gasping for breath, but she kept fighting. Thrashing, kicking, desperate to escape the pain in any way she could. I didn't think. I just reacted. I wrapped my arms around her, then my legs, locking her in, holding on for dear life, because that was exactly what was at stake.

She fought me with everything she had. But I wasn't letting go. I couldn't let go. And then finally she stopped. Not because she was okay. Not because I had saved her. Because she had nothing left to give. We collapsed together. Mentally. Physically. Emotionally wrecked. Two people, completely drained, drowning in the wreckage of what our lives had become.

A BREATH I DIDN'T DESERVE

And yet in the middle of all this torment, something shifted. As I held her, as the weight of everything crushed down on me, a truth I had refused to face finally broke through. I had spent years hating him. Blaming him. Carrying that resentment like a badge, convincing myself I was nothing like him. But in this moment, this unbearable, gut-wrenching moment, I saw the truth: I had become him. And for the first time, I understood him. I forgave him. Not for him. For me. And with that forgiveness, something inside me cracked open. The hatred, the resentment, the burden I had carried for so long, it lifted. And after many years, I could finally breathe. But even in the wake of that profound realization, even after releasing years of hatred, it wasn't enough. Not enough to save me. Not enough to pull me from the grip of my addiction.

By the very next day, I was right back where I started. Same vicious cycle. Same self-destruction. The insight should have been a turning point, a wake-up call. Instead, it was just another moment swallowed by the hunger. For weeks I lingered in that house, if you could still call it that. At that point it was just four walls and whatever scraps of my life were left.

Be honest: What part of your identity was built just to keep people from seeing the real you?

17

REHAB NO. 2: RED BOOTS AND RAW TRUTH

I showed up to the Care Unit Rehabilitation Center like the counselor from my first rehab said I would. Back then, I left against medical advice, thinking I knew better. As I walked out the door, he looked me dead in the eye and said, "If you leave, you'll be back. It may not be here, but it will be somewhere. And you will be telling the same stories as everyone else." I shrugged him off, thinking I was different. But here I was—same cycle, same pain, same stories.

By now I had lost everything—my job, my car, my home, my marriage, my self-esteem, and my dignity. I was barely holding on physically. If rock bottom had a basement, I was living in it. I didn't walk in with hope. I walked in because I had nowhere else to go.

During intake, they hit me with a surprise. My insurance wouldn't cover the drug unit. The only bed available was in the food disorder unit. I blinked at the nurse like she had to be joking. "Wait, what?" "We can place you in the food disorder unit," the nurse explained. "You'll eat and sleep with the food disorder patients, but you'll attend groups with the drug unit patients." I just stood there thinking, *You're putting the starving crackhead in a unit with people who have eating disorders, obesity, anorexia, and binge eating?* It felt like a twisted setup. But I agreed. I didn't have the strength to fight.

That first dinner was surreal. I walked into that dining hall like I'd just been released from solitary. I hit the buffet line hard. Fried chicken, lasagna, mashed potatoes, two thick slices of chocolate cake. Everyone else sat with color-coded, portion-controlled trays. Counting calories. No carbs. No sugars. I sat down with two plates big enough to feed a family and felt every eye in the room on me.

Then someone asked, "Jonathan . . . you gonna eat *all* that?" I smirked and tried to play it cool. "Hell yeah," I said. "Might die trying . . . but yeah." They laughed. But deep down it felt wrong. It seemed almost cruel to place those patients in that position. It was like asking me to detox in a crack house.

I was the only one who got to eat whatever I wanted, but I felt guilty loading up on comfort food in front of people trying to rebuild their relationship with eating. That night I sat in silence, eating every bite while a table full of strangers watched like I was the halftime show at a trauma convention. In the end, different addictions, same war.

After that, I kept quiet in group and just listened. And that was when the counselor's voice from the first rehab came back to me: "You'll be back . . . telling the same stories everyone else is telling." He was right. That hit hard. My life was humbled.

Eventually I found the courage to speak. I began to share things I had never said out loud. I talked about feeling abandoned whenever my father disappeared, how invisible I felt after my younger siblings were born, and the shame of poverty. And then the hardest truth: the molestation. I had repressed that for decades, swearing to never speak of it. But now I said it. My voice shook, but I let it out. It didn't free me all at once, but it cracked the door open a little further. It forced me to confront some of the unprocessed trauma I had been dragging behind me for years.

That led to the suggestion of bringing in my parents for family therapy day. I didn't know what I was hoping to get from it. I wasn't sitting there thinking, *Let's resolve my childhood trauma.* But I knew something inside me needed to be released, and they needed to hear it. My parents agreed to come. They didn't know what was about to hit them.

The room wasn't just us; it was filled with other patients and their families. About twenty-five people in a circle. It wasn't private. It wasn't safe. But it was real. Eyes forward, hearts tight. It was raw, public, and unfiltered.

When my turn came, I started with my mom. I was a mix of nerves, pain, anger, and resentment. I had long harbored these emotions, confused and hurt by my parents' actions during my childhood. I didn't have the words to unpack it all, but I had enough to speak the pain.

I told her I blamed her for pushing my dad out. That it felt like every argument ended with her saying, "Get out." As a kid, I couldn't make sense of any of it. I was just a child wanting his daddy. I didn't understand what was happening, only that one day he was there and the next he wasn't. Her voice could end everything in a heartbeat, even the safety that left the house with him.

Midway through my sentence, she snapped back, pointing at my father. "What about him?" I snapped back. "His turn is coming." She added, "You don't know what I went through." And she was right.

My mother was a five-foot-one, one-hundred-twenty-pound powerhouse born in Texas in 1935. By sixteen she was married with a child and raising her six siblings. By the time she had me at twenty-nine, she was already divorced once and now raising five kids. Her father left when she was nine, and she wouldn't see him again until she was thirty-eight. It wasn't just her father who left scars. Her mother did too. And those wounds?* They didn't stop with her. They came for me next. That's how generational pain works.

She protected her family from rats in the beds at night, sexual predators, abuse, and poverty. She learned early that no one was coming to save her. Survival was all she knew. So she became the one in charge. She didn't just lead the household—she commanded it. And everyone—cousins, siblings, uncles, kids—respected and feared her. I loved her, but I feared her too.

She carried masculine energy because she had to. She led when others folded. She didn't take shit from anyone. That was how she kept control. No patience for weakness. No time for excuses. So when she pushed my dad out? That was her way of surviving. But she wasn't just making a decision between adults; she was altering the safety of a child who didn't know how to explain the loss. That kind of rupture doesn't fade. It echoes.

---

* **The mother wound** is the emotional pain or unresolved trauma caused by a mother's absence, neglect, criticism, enmeshment, or inability to nurture and support her child in healthy, consistent ways. It often stems from a mother's own unhealed wounds—and can impact a child's sense of worth, safety, emotional expression, and ability to form secure relationships well into adulthood.

Important Distinction: *A mother wound doesn't only arise from overt abuse or abandonment. It can also stem from a mother who was physically present but emotionally unavailable, overly controlling, or consumed by her own pain. Even mothers who loved deeply but couldn't meet all their child's emotional needs can unintentionally pass down pain.*

I also brought up the moment I told her about the molestation and how her response hurt more than I ever admitted. She dismissed it and treated it like something shameful. Like something that should be buried. That moment didn't just hurt; it reinforced every fear I had, every reason I stayed silent all those years.

What I came to understand later was that my disclosure might have triggered her. She had survived her own childhood trauma, hiding in trees at twelve to avoid being molested by family members. She had sworn to protect us from the very thing that happened to her. My trauma added another layer to hers. It wasn't just my pain in the room that day. It was hers too.

Then I turned to my dad. I didn't let him off the hook. He had just heard me share something he never knew: the molestation. I saw the shock on his face. It was like he got hit with a truth he didn't know how to hold. We seldom had silence between us. But that moment, hearing something so raw, so unknown, put a weight in the space between us that neither of us knew how to hold. But now it had a name, and now it had weight.

I told him how disappointed I was. How abandoned I felt because he was barely around and when it counted most. I told him I knew he could have made different choices, ones that might have kept our family together. But my pops had his own shit too. He was born on a farm, one of eleven kids—eight brothers and two sisters. His parents were married for over sixty years, so what was his excuse? On the surface it looked like he came from stability. But he carried a father wound too. Damn. Guess I was bound to inherit his too.

I asked, "Why didn't you fight to stay? Why didn't you fight for me?" Then I gave him the memory that never left me. "I used to stand in the driveway at four o'clock every day, waiting for you to come home from work. I'd run to meet you, reach into your shirt pocket for Juicy Fruit or Life Savers, and I'd get disappointed when it was Rolaids." I smiled a little when I said it, but the pain underneath was no joke. "That was our thing," I said. "I looked forward to it. I looked forward to you. But then days went by . . . and you didn't come. And I got sad. Then weeks. Then months. And by that time I stopped looking."

The room was still quiet. Because this wasn't about candy. This was about presence. About a little boy who learned, way too young, that hope had an expiration date. What I didn't realize then was that the impact of my father wound would take years to fully understand. But at that moment, I was dealing with the shit right in front of me.

He looked at me and said, "I'm sorry, John. I didn't know how much I hurt you. I didn't know you were molested. And I am sorry, son." It didn't erase the past, but it meant something. Validation. Acknowledgment. I didn't sob, but I shed tears. For the kid who waited. For the man who carried that silence for decades. I didn't leave with closure, but I left lighter. Because for the first time, I let the pain speak.

After that family session, something in me shifted. Not a transformation but a crack in the wall. I was finally confronting some of the wounds I had been running from. And after a long time, I felt seen. There was distance between me and my mom for a time. We didn't talk much after that session. Too much had been said. Too much still sat between us, unspoken. But the silence was different this time. It wasn't avoidance. It was space. Space to feel. Space to think. Space to heal.

As the weeks rolled on, I got into a rhythm—meetings, meals, counseling, sharing war stories with other patients who knew what it meant to lose everything. I was getting stronger—physically, mentally, emotionally.

Melissa came to visit. She looked proud. She said she wanted to do something meaningful—something to celebrate my progress. It was something I'd always wanted: a motorcycle—a red, white, and blue Honda 550. We picked it out together on a day pass. I felt like a little kid with a new toy. But underneath that excitement, I was hiding something.

I'd been saving money. Every time someone gave me a few bucks for snacks or toiletries, I stashed it. I had nearly $300 tucked away. Not for groceries. Not for gas. For dope. See? While everyone else was preparing for my comeback, I was planning my comeback to the streets. I didn't tell a soul. I just smiled when they said how proud they were. I nodded during my final Cocaine Anonymous meeting when I got my thirty-day chip. I even stood up in front of the attendees and shared a little story, smiling as they clapped. Like I was all in. But inside? I already knew what I was doing the second I left those walls.

On my last night there, I barely slept. I lay in my bed staring at the ceiling, heart pounding, torn between guilt and craving. Part of me wanted to ask for help, to say "Hey, I'm scared. I don't trust myself." But I didn't. I didn't want to disappoint anyone—or maybe I didn't want anyone to stop me.

The next morning everyone lined up to hug me and say goodbye. Counselors smiled. Patients clapped. My motorcycle was already delivered, parked in front of the building like a symbol of freedom. Everyone thought I was riding off into a new life. And I was. Just not the life they imagined.

I walked out of rehab with shiny red boots, a clean thirty-day chip in my pocket, and the kind of smile people like to believe. I strapped on the helmet, hopped on the bike, and waved to everyone as I rolled out of the parking lot like some poster child for recovery.

Three hours later . . . I was high.

18

DEMONS DON'T KNOCK

I left rehab with a clean record and a dirty mind—a sobriety coin in my hand and a lie in my pocket. My demons were ready to greet me like old friends. Rehab gave me tools, but I never dropped the mask. I felt like an impostor, still armed with a match in one hand and a gas can in the other, preparing to blow my life up.

I knew the streets too well, and they knew me better than I liked to admit. My body was clean, but my mind was still locked in the same war. And the minute I felt freedom, I traded it for something familiar, even if that familiar thing was pain.

My wife, whom I was working to reconcile with, was living with her sister. I was homeless. We planned to stay at the hotel where I once worked. Walking back into a hotel room on my first day out of rehab was like stepping onto a minefield and calling it progress. That hotel wasn't a second chance—it was a setup. I had no business being there. Just thinking about the place during rehab stirred up cravings so strong I could taste them. My mouth would water, my heart would race, and I'd try to act like I was above it. I wasn't.

I told Melissa I'd meet her at the hotel after checking out of rehab. But I lied. I detoured on my brand-new bike and headed straight to the dope spot. I didn't even try to fight. I handed it all back. It was a full collapse in a single moment. The weight of what I'd lose hadn't hit me yet, but the guilt showed up fast, dragging shame in right behind it.

By the time I arrived at the hotel, high and ashamed, Melissa knew the moment she looked in my eyes. She looked at me with that combination of heartbreak and fury that only someone who's been burned too many times can pull off. She screamed at me with so much force it cracked something open inside me. I felt her pain like it was my pain.

She grabbed her things, turned around, and walked out. I tried to stop her, promising I wouldn't use again, but it was a lie. She got in the car, and I got on my motorcycle to follow her. Then she did something I didn't think she had in her: She hit the gas and rammed into the bike. I went flying off like a rag doll. My ass hit the pavement hard, and with the bike lying on top of me, she yelled, "Fuck you, Jonathan!" This was an "Oh shit, you had it coming, motherfucker" moment. Truthfully, I didn't know she had it in her. This gentle, caring woman I knew just showed me she wasn't taking my shit anymore. I had pushed her too far, mistaking her kindness for weakness. By the time I managed to pick myself up, bike on its side, back aching, pride shattered, she had already vanished. I was left with my tail between my legs, with nothing left to say. She was gone. And I deserved it.

That night I sat alone in the hotel room, puffing and puffing, staring at the ceiling, thinking about my progress and all the promises I'd made. It was the first time I was alone again since living in the empty house, and the weight of that isolation hit me harder than I expected. The feelings that night brought me to a dark place to maybe end it all.

In rehab, I had gained so much, one day at a time—sobriety, weight gain, self-esteem, trust, respect. And I didn't realize until that moment that I now had something to lose again. And it was all gone in one puff. The worst part wasn't the relapse. It was the knowing. The knowing that I planned it. That I wanted it. That I let it happen. I could still hear the counselor's voice in my head: "If you relapse, your life doesn't start from the first hit you ever took. You start where you left off." And damn if that wasn't true.

I had gone from a man with a plan to a man with nothing in less than four hours. No sobriety. No wife. No trust. Even the weight I had gained in rehab diminished within two weeks. I stopped eating, and the pounds fell off fast. And I didn't care.

I cashed in my motorcycle—sold it for $1,800, a sharp loss from the $3,000 we'd paid just weeks earlier. I told myself it was quick cash to get back on my feet. But let's be real—it just bought me more time to get high.

In a desperate bid to recoup funds, I ventured to the horse races, surprisingly winning $3,000. For someone else, that might've been a second chance. For me, it was a week of fuel to extend my binge.

By now, one month after discharge, I had burned every bridge, and somehow I still wanted more. I still thought I could turn it around with just one more hit. Just one more day. Just one more excuse.

Melissa had the car, her car, but I wanted it back. I needed transportation, a place to crash and to find the means to get high. I took a taxi to where she was staying and took the car. I still had keys. I didn't even knock. I just drove away, honking the horn like I'd won something.

Days later, lonely and scared, I called her. I needed to hear her voice. I wanted her to ask if I was okay, even though I wasn't. She didn't. She said what she needed to say. Cold. Distant. And I couldn't blame her. I'd run out of money, out of charm, out of gas—literally and figuratively.

All the money was gone. The lies had caught up. And all I had left was a question staring me in the face like a loaded gun: *Jonathan, how do you crawl out of this hole?* That was where I was, stuck in a cycle of toxicity. It didn't just hurt me; it hurt everyone around me. It drained my soul, hijacked my mind, and erased the little hope I had left. I was trapped in the clutches of my addiction, enslaved by a habit I could neither control nor escape.

What the hell was next?

19

JAILBIRD

You don't know yourself until freedom is gone. Jail didn't break me. I was already broken. What it did was put my broken pieces under a microscope—no distractions, no escape.

My sources of survival—money, a room, and the motorcycle—were gone, all smoked away. I had nothing but a handful of coins in my pocket and the rest of my life in bags, and even that felt like more than I deserved.

Desperate and delusional, I reached out to Melissa, hoping she would be willing to give me another chance. I called her sister's house and found out she was staying with my sister Candace. Yeah, *that* Candace. The one who had blamed me for Mirian's death. It felt like a slap to the face wrapped in betrayal, but I still convinced myself to go. I had to see what could come of it. Desperation clouds all human reasoning. Much to my surprise, despite our past tensions, my sister offered me a warm welcome, allowing me to stay with Melissa. Maybe I wasn't the villain in everyone's story. I accepted with hesitation.

Not surprisingly, our ceasefire broke after just one night. Melissa and I got into a fierce argument, old habits, old triggers, the same old pain. My sister, taking Melissa's side, ultimately kicked me out, just as I did her. It felt like vengeance, and I should have seen it coming. So I left, heartbroken, humiliated, and running on fumes, emotionally and literally.

Soon thereafter, sirens caught my attention, screaming behind me, the red and blue lights flashing in the rearview. I knew I was done. My driver's license was revoked eighteen months ago, and I was riding dirty with seven outstanding traffic warrants. No escape this time. Within minutes I was searched and arrested. I was terrified. This was the first time in my life I was going to jail. A whole new level of intense disappointment in myself started to set in as I was being handcuffed and placed in the back of the squad car. I was booked, fingerprinted, and stripped of what little dignity I had left. *If survival had a soundtrack, mine skipped a beat the moment that cell door slammed shut.*

It was there that I learned it was my sister who reported me to the police. She called saying I had stolen my wife's car. She gave them everything—the revoked license, the warrants, the whole play-by-play. If I had just stayed away, if I had gone anywhere else, would I still be free right now? That betrayal. It cut deeper than any jail cell ever could. And yet I wasn't surprised. That was the real pain.

Following a night in jail, I was informed of my impending transfer to the Inglewood courthouse. Bound in shackles and filled with confusion, my future looked bleak as I was loaded onto a bus known on the streets as the "Grey Goose." During my first court appearance, I faced three outstanding traffic warrants, each one carrying a three-day jail sentence. I had already served one night, but that didn't make the road ahead feel any shorter.

The booking process at Los Angeles County Jail was nothing short of degrading. I endured a full strip search, followed by a harsh delousing shower that destroyed my Jheri curl, leaving my shag cut a frizzy, puffed-out mess. Then came another blow to what little self-respect I had left: I was told to throw my underwear in the middle of the floor. Apparently, my old-school briefs without the front fly weren't jail-approved. That left me without any underwear for the remainder of my incarceration—just the stiff, scratchy jumpsuit rubbing against the crack of my ass, stripping away the last shreds of dignity I had left.

I found myself in an overcrowded dormitory where sleep was a luxury no one could afford. I kept my shoes and socks on to avoid theft, a small act of self-preservation in a place where everything could be taken from you. Eventually I was relocated to a shared cell, where my bed was nothing more than a cold metal bunk, no mattress, no pillow, just steel and silence.

As the weekend dragged on, my health started to spiral. Whether it was drug withdrawals, illness, or just the weight of everything collapsing at once, my body gave out. Bedridden and neglected, I suffered chills, fever, and sweats in silence, invisible to the world and forgotten by the system. And if that wasn't enough, I went all six days without taking a single dump. Not one. The buildup was massive, physically and mentally. There was just something about that open toilet in full view of everyone that made my bowels shut down. My body was screaming, but my pride refused to sit. Jail will mess with your head, but it'll mess with your gut too.

On Monday, two additional court appearances resulted in the three remaining warrants being added to my sentence, leaving me confined three more days to my jail cell in a disheveled, dirty state. Finally, I was able to contact my wife to inform her of my upcoming release. Her voice betrayed no signs of concern or empathy. *Some birds sing in cages. I sat in silence, wings clipped by choices I swore I'd never make.* I wasn't locked up for a long time, but it was long enough to meet the version of me I'd been avoiding.

Released at five in the morning, I didn't have a plan. No ride, no home, no money, just the early morning air and a pair of busted shoes and smelly socks on my feet. I wandered aimlessly through downtown LA, clutching forty-five cents in my hand like it was gold. But it wasn't enough for breakfast, a bus ride, or even a real phone call.

I didn't try calling anyone at first. I wasn't even sure who'd pick up. Shame kept me quiet, and pride kept me moving. I roamed the city for hours, block after block, through alleys, past bus stops, and alongside people sleeping on cardboard boxes. By late afternoon reality hit me harder than any jail sentence. My body was exhausted, and my spirit crushed. That was when I finally decided to try JR, my childhood best friend since the age of ten. He lived in a modest downtown hotel and was the closest thing I had to safe harbor. I found a payphone and dropped in twenty cents. No answer. That left me with a single quarter and the streets beneath my feet. With nowhere to go and no one to turn to, I strolled the city for hours, dazed, dirty, and disoriented. I wasn't just witnessing homelessness. I was living it. *I was caged—not by bars this time but by failure, shame, and the consequences of my own choices.*

JR was my only real option and was like a brother to me. I started making my way toward his building, slow and unsteady, hoping I could find him after his shift. There was no guarantee he'd say yes, not with my track record, but I had to try. As I walked, I realized I felt no different or looked no different than the homeless people I passed. Our steps, our faces, our struggle—there was no difference.

Is this where I really belonged? I thought. The city didn't see me. I blended in with the invisible. I looked like a homeless man because I was. I moved like an addict because I was. The only difference now was I couldn't lie to myself anymore. And once you see yourself for real, you can't unsee it. Not even if you tried.

20

PATHETIC THIEF

As I arrived outside JR's hotel, I stumbled into the phone booth to call one last time. My hands trembled as I dropped my final quarter into the payphone—the very last piece of control I had left. When I called, I'd reach the hotel operator first. She would ring his room, and with each pause, my anxiety deepened. Each ring on the other end felt like an eternity, tightening the grip of panic around my chest. When JR finally answered, the relief hit me like a wave, crashing hard against the fear of being rejected. I exhaled the breath I didn't know I was holding. I quickly informed him that I was outside and that I was hoping to ask if I could stay with him a few days. He said, "Man, yeah . . . come on, JC, you know it's okay," and reassured me he would come down.

The room was the kind that you paid for weekly and was furnished with a bed, chair, and TV. That evening the exhaustion hit me like a brick wall. I was beyond hungry—my body craving fuel, my spirit craving rest. JR, always showing up when I needed it most, left to grab me a burger and fries. When he came back, I devoured the food like I hadn't eaten in weeks. In truth I hadn't. But my stomach could only handle so much. After days of no bowel movements, my insides were still in chaos, trying to process whatever little I could keep down. The greasy taste of the burger lingered as I lay back, finally full—but still empty. I crashed hard, right there on the floor at the foot of his bed. It was the first real sleep I'd had in days.

At five o'clock the following morning, JR, dressed for work, confronted me anxiously. He asked me, "JC, am I going to come back and find all my shit is gone?" His words cut me deep, almost bringing me to tears, but I swallowed the lump in my throat and promised him that I wouldn't touch his belongings. He retorted, "It's not the old JC I'm concerned about. It's the Jonathan on drugs who I'm worried about. That dude may steal my shit." His words were a painful reminder of the trust and integrity I had lost, but I assured him again that his things would be safe.

After JR left for work, I discarded my worn-out shoes and socks—shoes that had been on my feet since the day I was booked into LA County Jail. Eight days of funk clung to them, soaked through with athlete's foot, sweat, and shame. The stench was foul, a mix of sour body odor and despair. Even I couldn't ignore it anymore.

Before stepping into the shower, I used the ten dollars JR had left to buy a laxative. It was a strange priority, but after eight days of my system being locked up, I needed the release. When it finally kicked in, I felt physically lighter but still mentally wrecked. It's an odd sensation, purging waste while still carrying the emotional weight of rock bottom.

Then I took a long-needed shower, watching the grime wash away in slow spirals down the drain. As the hot water hit my skin, it was more than just cleansing—it was a baptism of desperation. My tears mixed in with the stream, unnoticed. I leaned into the wall, letting the water soak me to the bone, hoping it could scrub off the guilt that had clung to me for weeks. The stench of sweat and hopelessness began to lift, but the emotional grime stuck harder. Still, in that moment, I let it all fall—grief, regret, and everything else I was holding on to.

Thankfully, my wife came through on her promise to drop off fresh clothes and shoes I had in the car. And as I took a pair of dull scissors and began cutting off the remnants of my Jheri curl, it felt less like grooming and more like shedding a piece of my old self. I had held on to that curl longer than I should have, hoping—somewhere deep inside—that if I could just get my look back, maybe I could get my swag back too. But holding on to it was like holding on to a lie, pretending I could return to a version of me that no longer existed. Each snip was a silent declaration—I can't go back there. The hair fell in clumps, littering the floor like fragments of my broken pride. It was symbolic, a desperate attempt to cut ties with the version of me that had spiraled so far out of control.

Knowing I couldn't stay with JR much longer, I turned to my father. His two-bedroom, one-bathroom apartment was already full, as my older brother Jonas and my sixteen-year-old brother Tony were also living there. He kept a small motor home parked right outside the apartment and, with undeserved kindness, offered it to me. It wasn't much, but to me it was everything—a small, contained sanctuary amid the storm brewing in my life. He gave me keys to the apartment to come in for showers and food when needed. That simple gesture meant more than he probably realized. I hadn't earned it, but he gave it anyway. At this point, not due to my own accord, I was two weeks sober. My jail confinement and being dead broke had forced me into it.

Then came the fateful day my father sent me out with twenty dollars to get fried chicken from KFC. That money might as well have been a loaded weapon in my pocket because the moment it touched my hand, the craving lit up in my body like wildfire. I couldn't tell you if it was a test on his part, but if it was, I failed it faster than a heartbeat. I didn't even try to fight it. Instead of fried chicken, I bought rock cocaine. The high didn't hit fast enough to numb the guilt or drown out the holy fear of having to look my father in the face afterward. That fear came from the very real possibility of getting the shit knocked out of me. I had always feared my dad's hands. Though he stood only five feet, seven inches tall, his ring finger was a size 18. His pinky? Probably the size of my thumb. You didn't mess around with a man like that. I had crossed plenty of lines before, but this time felt different.

Returning home the following morning, I knew I'd be alone. But before that, I took Melissa's car while she was at work. I still had a set of keys, so I didn't need permission. I didn't show up or ask; I just got in and drove off. Later, I called her from a payphone to let her know. She cried. I didn't care. I was too far gone for guilt. In an act of desperation, I broke into my father's locked bedroom and stole his TV and checkbook, as well as Tony's keyboard, the same keyboard he played at church. A pawnshop, a grocery store for check cashing, and a few hundred dollars later, I was back at the drug house. This was my life, spiraling downward in a destructive cycle of cravings, theft, and drugs.

Just days later came a chance encounter with my brother Jonas outside a grocery store. Cornered, with nowhere to run, I braced myself for an ass whipping. Jonas was furious, demanding answers about the missing keyboard and TV. The fury in his eyes gave way to a pained confusion as I handed him the pawn slip. My actions had torn a gaping hole in our relationship. They could have called the police and sent me back to jail, adding the title of felon to the ever-growing list of names I never asked for but fully earned.

Pinned against the wall and face-to-face, Jonas just looked at me, and with disgust and a tone I had never heard before, he said, "Everyone's trying to give you a chance, but you have really fucked up now. You'll never be trusted as far as I'm concerned, and I will never claim you as my brother." His words, sharp as daggers, cut me. But not enough. The lingering high made me invincible against his accusations. He walked away, unaware of the extent of my deception.

My mind spun as I scrambled for a next move. I was out of options but not out of hustle. I needed a place to stay, to rest, to get high—and fast. Then it came to me: the hotel I had once worked at. A place where no one knew my current situation. Where I still had a little credibility left. So maybe, just maybe, I could pull something off there.

I reached out to a former colleague, who was now managing the hotel. Our conversation was casual, even friendly, but underneath, I had an agenda. When he asked how he could help, I explained my fabricated story: "I've been traveling and working with my dad. I need a room for a few days. Can you help?" Without hesitation, he welcomed me in, even agreeing to accept a check from my dad as payment. Once I arrived, I was given a suite. Familiar with the hotel's practices from my past employment, I asked to cash a check. I wrote it for one hundred dollars, claiming it had been presigned by my dad. No questions asked, just cash. For a moment, I had a roof, some money, and the illusion that I still had control.

The hotel, about twenty-five miles outside of LA, turned into my temporary fortress, a base for frequent drug runs. I wasn't thinking clearly. Addiction had a choke hold on my logic. Instead of planning bigger, more strategic hits, I clung to small, quick forty-dollar pickups that barely scratched the itch. Every trip back was a gamble. By day five, paranoia crept in like smoke under the door. I knew the jig was almost up. The checks would eventually bounce, or worse, my dad would notice and stop payment. I tried to be slick, cashing them during different shifts, but it was only a matter of time before someone caught the mismatch—Jonas Crawford Sr. on the checks, Jonathan Crawford on the ID. The clock was ticking, and I could hear it in every knock on the door.

On the sixth day, I saw the general manager eyeing my room and noting my car's license plate. My stomach sank. It was a clear sign that the curtain was about to fall. I knew the consequences were closing in—police involvement and potential charges from my dad. I had to leave. I had violated his space, stolen his belongings, and forged about fifteen of his checks. That was more than a mistake; it was betrayal.

This moment brought a stark realization: The real enemy wasn't the lies I told or the scams I pulled; it was addiction. A thief of truth. A master manipulator that rewired my loyalty and wrecked every relationship I had. I hadn't just stolen money; I had stolen trust, love, and hope from the people who still believed in me. Unintentionally, I'd turned my father into an enabler, someone who unknowingly funded the very destruction he prayed I'd escape. I had exploited his love and trust to sustain my addiction, entrenching us both in a damaging cycle that seemed impossible to break. The suite I stayed in, the fake comfort of the drugs, it was all just smoke covering the wreckage. I wasn't living. I was disappearing. Piece by piece, breath by breath. Suffocating in the very addiction I once thought I had under control, only to realize it had been controlling me all along. Something had to give. And eventually it did.

If you're ready, write about a moment you're still ashamed of—but from the perspective of someone who forgives you. Then ask: What lesson did I steal from that experience?

21

REHAB NO. 3: THE PSYCHO SCENE

You'd think after crashing this many times I'd stop being surprised, but when I looked around at the mess my life had become, I still caught myself asking, *How the hell did I get here?* I already knew the answer.

Addiction doesn't just steal your money or your relationships. It robs you of logic. And here I was—starving, strung out, and hiding in South Central LA, still trying to chase a high that didn't even feel good anymore. My car became my home. My sanctuary. My prison.

I called my mom in desperation. Despite everything between us, she gave me twenty dollars. I told myself I'd buy food. I didn't. Three bucks went to gas, two dollars went to cheap hot dogs, and the rest went straight to my habit. Coming down was hell. The paranoia, the racing heart, and the anxiety made my skin itch. Then I would curl up in that little Datsun, tossing and turning until I passed out from sheer exhaustion. I'd wake to the blistering sun, drained and unsure of what to do next. I saved my parking spot as a refuge and wandered around aimlessly, hunger buried beneath the taste of crack. This self-destructive cycle lasted forty-eight days.

My physical health deteriorated right alongside everything else. I was dehydrated and malnourished. My body was giving out, but my addiction didn't care. I survived on leftovers and melted ice water. One night I gathered the strength to drive to a gas station to drink water from the radiator filling station. Not bottled water. Not a fountain. Radiator water.

Afterward, I sat there in the car, engine off, silence loud. I couldn't remember the last time I ate a full meal. I couldn't remember the last time I truly laughed. I couldn't even remember the last time I took a shower, combed my hear, or brushed my teeth. The fear. The pain. The loneliness. The confusion. I was cracked open, raw, and exposed. That was when the tears came. Heavy and relentless. I broke.

I bowed, hands shaking, heart pounding. And I started to whisper, then cry, then plead. *Dear Lord . . . help me. Please help me, Lord. Lord, please help me. Help me. Help me, please. I don't know what to do. I don't know where to go. Who is this inside of me? I'm tired. I'm scared. I'm ashamed. I've lost everything . . . I need you now.* I wasn't bargaining. I didn't have anything left to bargain with. I was begging. I wasn't asking for a miracle. I wasn't even sure I believed one could happen. I just wanted a lifeline. A sign. All I had left was prayer, and that night I gave it everything I had.

Returning to my spot, I realized the enormity of my situation and said to myself, "If you can overcome this, Jonathan, there isn't anything you couldn't do. This *will* be the hardest thing you'll ever have to overcome." I began to see the mountain I had to climb. Part of me wanted to give up, but another part knew I had nothing left to lose.

At 2:00 a.m., I walked six blocks to a nearby phone booth. The streets of South Central were empty. My hope was hanging by a thread. I started making collect calls to every rehab center in the phone directory. One after another. I hit walls, no beds, no room, no callbacks. Finally, one said yes. They asked if I could get there. I told the truth: I didn't have enough gas in my car to make it across town. *When survival becomes your only priority, pride has no place.*

They arranged a taxi. I packed up what little I had—my belongings, my dirty clothes, my broken spirit—and left the car behind. When the cab pulled up, I climbed in, silent. The driver looked at me through the rearview mirror. "You okay?" I stared out the window for a beat, then said the only thing I could: "No."

This time was different.

Rehab no. 2 was painful, but I still had things to prove. I walked out with fresh red boots, a tough exterior, and the belief that I could talk my way through recovery. I wasn't ready. I was still clinging to my ego and trying to control the outcome.

Rehab no. 3? All that was stripped away. I walked in broken. I was a shell of a man, barely 120 pounds of bones. A former inmate. Kicked out of my sister's house. Robbed my dad. Living out of my car for two months, with no shower, no food, not even toothpaste. *I wasn't ready to be healed, but I was tired of being broken.*

I wasn't walking into rehab. I was crawling in with whatever was left of me. I would spend Halloween, Thanksgiving, Christmas, New Year's, and my twenty-third birthday inside those walls. There were no parties. No cake. No celebration. Just a room, group meetings, and the sobering reminder of how far I'd fallen. And even in that controlled environment, even surrounded by support, I still relapsed within the first month. I was granted a short four-hour leave, and I used. That was how deep this shit was. Even safety couldn't stop the craving. Even structure couldn't stop the sabotage. But this time I came back. Not just physically—I came back mentally.

But change doesn't happen in straight lines, and I still had more breaking to do. Even after relapsing, I tried to hold on to control in my own twisted way. I smuggled in actual coffee. Caffeinated coffee wasn't even allowed in the facility, so bringing it in was already breaking the rules. Then a landline phone. I brought it in so I wouldn't have to wait for the payphone. I'd talk on it late into the night, falling asleep mid-conversation like I was safe in my own bed at home. It was absurd—and part of me knew it—but in that moment it gave me a false sense of normalcy, a hint of comfort I hadn't felt in months. I'd wake up with the receiver still resting against my chest, the dial tone humming like a lullaby. Somehow I had convinced myself I belonged in both worlds—recovery by day, deception by night. Not just hiding them in my room, plugging the phone into the wall like it was no big deal. Like I could balance recovery and secrecy in the same breath.

One morning I woke up to whispers. The overnight staff had spotted the phone lying next to me during room checks, as I slept with the receiver still in hand. Panic set in. I scrambled to stash the phone outside my window, desperate to erase the evidence. But it was too late. They shut the whole place down. Every room was searched. Every patient was punished for my mess. I didn't just break the rules. I broke trust. I brought chaos into a space meant for making change. The old patterns, the lies, the sneaking, and the self-sabotage were alive and well. And if I didn't kill them, they were going to kill me.

So I did something I had never done before: I owned it. I admitted to everything—the coffee, the phone, the deception. I didn't fight the consequences. I took the heat. And I didn't just stop there. I got serious. I started participating more in groups, showing up early, staying late, checking in on others, doing the quiet work no one saw but everyone felt. And that was when something unexpected happened: They made me patient president. Imagine that—my first leadership role was in rehab. Me, the guy who caused a lockdown. The same one who just relapsed weeks ago. It didn't feel like a reward. It felt like a challenge, a chance to lead by example, not by perfection. I had to be accountable, not only for myself but also for everyone in that facility. I had to show up every day with honesty, humility, and the grit to try again.

That responsibility saved me. It gave me structure. It gave me purpose. And for the first time, I started seeing myself as something more than just an addict trying to survive. With that new responsibility came something else: clarity. The more I showed up for others, the more I realized how badly I wanted to show up for the people I'd hurt most. I wasn't just trying to lead inside those walls—I was trying to heal what I hoped was waiting for me outside of them.

Melissa agreed to counseling, hoping to mend the wounds my addiction had caused. Our relationship had weathered the storm of addiction, but the pathway to normalcy was still under construction. Truth be told, I wasn't sure if I was reconciling out of love or security. Maybe it was both. Maybe neither. But it was a start.

My step-kids joined some of the counseling sessions during my stay. My stepdaughter was quick to forgive. She still saw something in me worth holding on to. My stepson? He wasn't having it, and I couldn't blame him. He'd watched me tear his world apart. The pain I inflicted on his mother and witnessing my self-destruction had left deep scars. He was justifiably angry and hurt, feelings that he openly expressed. He didn't want to live with me, and that one cut deep. Our counselor, understanding the delicate situation, suggested that my stepson move in with his aunt for the time being. I knew he needed space. And maybe I needed to prove, without words, that I had changed.

In the middle of all that growth, something happened that shook me to my core. During one of our group sessions, the psychotherapist looked at me and asked, "Are you ready to really work on your childhood wounds?" I said yes, but I had no idea what I was agreeing to. They called it a psychodrama. I called it a setup. I didn't know it was going to feel like an exorcism—the Holy Ghost and a breakdown rolled into one. It wasn't just therapy—it was a psychological ambush, designed to drag out everything you've buried and make you fight for the right to heal.

He told me to take off my shoes, lie down in the center of the room, and close my eyes. Then he had others gather close, some were told to hold down my arms and legs. Then he lit the fuse. He stepped into the role of my mother, channeling her voice, her tone, her coldness. He didn't just say what she never said. He made me feel the weight she never could carry. His voice came sharp and aggressive. "You can't be ten anymore. You can't be a child. Grow the fuck up."

He dragged my trauma to the surface and called out the molestation, the silence, the shame, the helplessness. He kept pushing. "Are you a man or a little fucking victim?" The anger surged. I started crying. Then shaking. Then screaming. The others joined in, playing their roles: "Be a man, little boy." "You're too weak to get up." I fought like hell. Thrashing. Screaming. Sobbing. Trying to break free. But they held me down. And as I lay there, buried in rage and pain, I noticed something: Everyone in the room was filled with emotions, crying, sobbing. They saw my pain. They *felt* it. Some had to be comforted because it triggered their own trauma. The entire room was pulled into the drama. And I was the damn guinea pig.

When it was over, I was wrecked. Physically drained. Emotionally raw. Spiritually stripped. But something had been released. I wasn't healed, but it broke something that needed to break. I had begun to let go of something that had haunted me for years. And I wasn't the only one wrecked. Every patient in that room was shattered by what they had witnessed. There were hugs. Tears. People being comforted who weren't even part of the exercise—it triggered something deep in all of us.

At dinner that night, no one spoke. Everyone sat in silence, eyes swollen, plates barely touched. That room had seen something sacred and brutal. And none of us walked away the same. For the first time, the pain wasn't just mine to carry anymore.

I spent over three months in rehab, and as my discharge approached, I faced the reality of my past and the future I was working toward. My life was defined not by my addiction but by my recovery and the person I was becoming. I had the serenity to accept the things I could not change, the courage to change the things I could, and the wisdom to know the difference.

But did I really?

Inside rehab, I had structure. I had support. I had people holding me accountable. I had a safe space to say no. But outside, the world wasn't padded with check-ins and counselors. It was real and unpredictable. And I didn't know yet if the version of me that could thrive in rehab could survive outside it.

For the first time in two years and four months, I was seventy days sober. That might not sound like much to most people, but for me, it was everything. I had fought for every single one of those days. But sobriety in rehab is one thing. Sobriety in the real world? That's where the real fight begins. I knew I needed a sponsor. I knew I needed meetings. I knew all the things they tell you to do, and I knew how easy it was to talk yourself out of doing them. I started slipping. Missing meetings. Convincing myself I could handle it on my own. Lying to myself again.

Eventually I relapsed, and the guilt came rushing back like an old friend. I traded personal items for drugs. I even gave up my bike for a hit and walked eight miles home stoned, ashamed, and furious with myself. I had made it past a hundred days, and just like that, I was back to square one. But even in my failure, I held on to "*If I can stop this, there isn't anything I can't do.*" That line became my lifeline. Because even though I stumbled, I had changed. And this time I was learning how to fight back.

Ask yourself: What truth hurt the most to see—but freed you the most once you did?

22

HOW DID I GET HERE? PART 2

The most dangerous lies are the ones we tell ourselves. I faked my own suicide. And I still ended up in the psych ward. That alone should tell you how far gone I was. The day I told my wife I was going to kill myself and the amount of shit that followed is still hard to sit with. I was a master manipulator. I had lied so well even I believed it sometimes. That's when you know you're fucked up.

They admitted me to the locked unit first. I had no shoestrings, no belt. I was stripped of everything, including the last shred of pride I'd been holding on to. The first morning in the unit was a vivid reminder of a very long night I had spent dealing with my roommate. I was engulfed in fear, repeating to myself, "What have I done? How did I get here?" This marked my fourth time going into a facility, with three rehab stints and now this psychiatric unit, all part of a journey that saw me voluntarily surrendering my freedom. The sight of people aimlessly walking around, banging their heads against walls, and stumbling over my stuff provoked an internal inquiry, a constant "Why?"

That morning brought a brief relief when I was moved from the tight confines of the lockdown unit to an open one. Finally, they had the bed available that they had promised. Suddenly, things were looking better; the new setting was more like a resort. Positioned on the top floor of this high-rise hospital, the room offered an expansive view, a visual treat that accompanied the three meals a day. My day-to-day routine included a variety of activities. However, interspersed within these activities was a heavy dose of psychiatric counseling and therapy.

I had faked that suicide attempt. I had pretended to swallow the pills in front of my wife. It was one lie after another that led to a dramatic sequence of events: my wife calling the neighbor for help, both dragging me down the stairs, me playing deadweight, and eventually getting transported to the hospital. Even at the hospital, it was all an act. I knew how to relax myself for the sake of lowering my heart rate. The fear of getting my stomach pumped made me drink charcoal, a substance meant to dilute the drugs I had supposedly taken. *When your lies become your lifeline, you've officially lost your grip on reality.* Looking back, I realized my performance was Oscar-worthy.

How could I admit this to my wife, let alone myself? So I continued with the treatment, day after day, week after week. She would come to visit each day, or every other day, and I would maintain the pretense, acting as though I had genuinely attempted to take my life. But I was an impostor, still acting the role of a fool, thinking I had gotten over. On the outside I was improving. On the inside? My guilt was still on lockdown. And just like that, the mask started to crack.

They called my wife and suggested she attend a family therapy session with me. And she came. I remember the moment she walked in, eyes heavy, spirit even heavier. She sat across from me, and we were asked to talk. Talk? About what? "Do you have anything you want to say?" the therapist asked. I looked at her, then at my wife. "I don't even know where to begin." She didn't flinch. She just looked . . . empty. I had nothing to say that wouldn't crumble whatever tiny bit of foundation was left between us. I started mumbling half apologies and fragmented sentences, hoping for some grace. Instead, I got silence. Not cold silence. Just . . . depleted. She was all out of energy. And honestly, I couldn't blame her.

The people around me in the unit were fighting their own battles. Some were worse. My roommate, Irv—a sixty-year-old man—was undergoing electric shock treatments. Watching him go through that added another layer of reality to the whole experience. I had mastered the art of playing the victim—until I became one for real. Who among us had faked their suicide and stayed in treatment as if it had happened?

I used to give motivational talks in the mirror, dressed sharp, rehearsing for the life I swore I'd build. Now I was rehearsing my lies in hospital scrubs. At night I'd lie awake wondering how I had become this person. How I went from being full of ambition to damn near being strapped to a hospital bed for observation. It didn't happen overnight, but it sure felt like it.

Day 30 came, and just like that, I was discharged. Still asking "How did I get here?" I was painfully aware that I could never tell anyone about just how low I would stoop to prove I was, in fact, the victim.

That little boy who only had me to protect him, yeah, he was still around. Still watching. Still waiting to be seen. Still waiting for an adult to carry his load. Still wondering, *How did we even get here?*

PART III

THE SHIFT—WHERE MOMENTUM IS BORN

Momentum wasn't a miracle. It was a decision I had to make in motion.

23

UNBEARABLE

Melissa had been distant for days, her eyes carrying something heavy, something she wasn't saying. And then one evening she finally did. "I'm pregnant." The words hit me like a tidal wave—unexpected, powerful, impossible to ignore. For a moment I couldn't breathe. After everything, after all the chaos, she was giving me news that should have been a moment of hope, but instead, it terrified me. I wanted to be happy. I wanted to believe this would change everything. But I was scared.

Melissa had already endured five miscarriages, each one chipping away at her hope, my hope, our hope. When she told me she was pregnant, we were hesitant to believe it could last. Despite the history, our history, I tried. We both did. Every doctor's appointment, bed rest, cautious step, we held our breath, hoping this time would be different. And for months it was. She made it further than ever before. The fourth month. Then the fifth. It felt like maybe, just maybe, we were finally winning against the odds. But we had been here before. Each pregnancy had felt like a fragile wish, one that fate had cruelly taken from us time and time again. This moment felt like standing on the edge of a cliff, waiting for the fall.

Then one night, the scream.

Melissa's scream shattered the silence. The kind of scream that wasn't just from physical pain—it carried history, remembrance, and raw fear. The moment her water broke, everything around us dissolved, and for a brief second, I felt like I wasn't standing in that bedroom—I was inside Melissa's memory, inside her past. Her daughter, my stepdaughter, was born premature at six months. She had spent an entire year in the hospital, enduring multiple surgeries. That was the weight Melissa carried when she screamed. The past and the present collapsed into each other in that one sound.

She clutched her stomach and cried out for help, pleading to use the bathroom. The paramedics had just arrived when she staggered in, gripping me and the sink for support. The moment she sat, there was a splash. A sound so final, so wrong that my mind refused to comprehend it. I rushed to help her up, her body trembling, her eyes wide with the kind of terror you don't come back from. And then I saw him.

My son.

Lifeless. Helpless. Defenseless. Sitting in the toilet water. No crying. No tears. No movement.

Everything in me shattered. I stood there, frozen, my breath caught somewhere in my chest. His body, so small, so still, emerged, as if he were waiting for me. His eyes were closed, but in my mind I imagined them staring at me, looking up as if he knew. Knew that I had failed. Knew that, in some twisted way, I might be the reason he never took a breath.

Melissa sobbed, her body convulsing with grief, but I barely moved. All I could do was stare. My legs felt cemented to the floor. My mind screamed at me to do something, to grab him, to save him, but reality had already declared its verdict. I wasn't meant to save him. He was already gone.

The paramedics arrived, their movements fast and precise, but their faces carried none of the urgency I wanted to see. They lifted him and unwrapped the umbilical cord from around him, and without hesitation, without even a second of hope, they cut it. They detached our son, as if he had never belonged to us at all. As if he had only ever belonged to death.

I wanted to scream. To shake them. To demand they try. Why weren't they trying? He wasn't an embryo. He had fingers, toes, dark curls. He had a face. But he didn't have a chance.

We were rushed to the hospital together, but it didn't feel real. I held Melissa's hand as she wept, as she whispered apologies to our son as if she had done something wrong. As if either of us had. The room smelled like sickness and antiseptic, the walls closing in around us. My hands gripped the arms of the chair so hard my hands clenched involuntarily, tension rippling through my fingers. The bathroom, the sight of the water, the sound of the splash—none of it left my mind. It followed me everywhere.

No one asked if we wanted a funeral. No one brought it up. And neither did we. The idea of planning a service—choosing a casket, standing over a grave, speaking his name out loud—was unthinkable. The thought never even made it to the surface. It was buried in our pain, just as he was.

The sorrow I should have embraced, it didn't settle in my chest. It lodged itself in Melissa's grief. And in the drugs I inhaled. I couldn't understand the magnitude of her pain, having carried our son, the bond they shared. So I numbed it the only way I knew how. I inhaled until the images blurred, until the sounds of Melissa's scream faded into the background, until the weight of guilt, of failure, of unbearable loss became nothing but a whisper.

But even in my highest moments, he was always there. Floating. Watching. Wondering why his father had let him go. His dad, a drug addict who had been to three rehabs and a psychiatric unit and staged a suicide. I did everything—from selling toilets to living on the streets. What kind of role model could I have been for him? The cumulative weight of the now five miscarriages and a stillbirth, compounded by the traumatic memory of my sister's suicide and the dark revelations of molestation, pushed me deeper into my addiction.

And then I had to go home. Back to the bathroom, the blood, the amniotic fluid soaking the bedsheets, the trail leading from the bedroom to where our son had taken his first and only moment in this world. I scrubbed the floor, my tears mixing with the water and disinfectant, as if I could cleanse away the horror. With every wipe of the floor, every scrub of the toilet, I cried. And then came the final act—the moment I had to flush. My hands trembled as I reached for the handle, and as the water swirled, it felt like I was flushing his life away. I stood there, staring, unable to move, unable to breathe, consumed by the crushing reality that this was all that was left of him. Just water. Just silence.

Try this: Draw a line down the middle of a page. On the left, list what you lost. On the right, list what you gained from surviving it. Let both be true.

24

HOPE

Seven months later I experienced the most monumental breakthrough of my life: *I was exhausted.* Not just physically but also mentally and emotionally. Every fiber of my being felt worn thin. My body had betrayed me, my mind had deceived me, and my soul had been screaming for a reprieve I had ignored for far too long. Every inhale felt heavy, like I was breathing in regret. Every exhale was a reminder of the years lost to this addiction.

I sat on the cold tile floor, my eyes swollen from crying, my back against the wall, knees pulled up to my chest. My head throbbed. My body ached in ways I couldn't explain. My stomach twisted, threatening to turn itself inside out, but there was nothing left to purge. I had spent the last few hours bent over a toilet, dry-heaving, my body rejecting every ounce of poison I had once welcomed with open arms.

I stared at the cracks in the ceiling, as if they were the crack I smoked. How did I let it get this far? I had seen this drug strip people bare—steal their souls, turn their bodies frail, leave their minds empty shells. But I had fed myself the same lie so many before me had swallowed whole: "Not me. I'm stronger than that." Turns out, the lie was stronger than me.

The weight of every decision, every misstep, every failure caught up to me. My hands trembled as I pressed them against my temples, desperate to quiet the pounding headache and the relentless nausea. I felt panic attacks every hour, one crashing into the next, leaving me gasping for air and gripping reality.

"I can't do this anymore," I whispered to myself. My voice cracked, raw from dehydration and desperation. The silence answered back. There was no one left to talk me down, no one left to lie to. Just me. And the truth. My life was fucked up.

A shiver ran through me, not just from the withdrawal but also from the revelation creeping into my bones: The fear of staying stuck in this addiction, this life, this story was greater than the fear of going through withdrawals, of feeling the pain I had tried so hard to bury.

I exhaled sharply. "Who am I if not my addiction?" The question hovered in the air, unanswered. I had built my identity around the high, around the chase, around the numbing. Without it, I was just a man—a broken man.

But maybe that was enough this time. Was this the actual bottom I heard so much about? The bottom I thought I had hit several times over? I didn't want to die like this. But more than that, I wanted to live.

This breakthrough came with another chilling realization: *The pain would never go away, but I could have the pain and manage it with a healthy state of mind.* I could carry it without letting it consume me. The past would not change, but my future, that was still unwritten.

For the first time, hope wasn't some far-off, abstract concept. It was here. It was real. It wasn't a grand revelation. I had a choice. And after a long time, I chose me. I pressed my palms against the ground and slowly pushed myself up, unsteady but determined.

The withdrawals came in relentless waves, each one punishing me for the way I abused myself. Cold sweat slicked my back, the air around me feeling too thick to breathe, but this time was different.

There were no structured days, no group therapy sessions, no staff making sure I stayed clean. Rehab had always given me a script to follow, a system that allowed me to believe I was getting better. The first rehab, I was in denial. The second, I played the game, knowing my cravings became stronger each day. The third, I swore it was for good until I stepped outside, and the weight of reality flattened me. Rehab hadn't failed me. I had failed me.

Now there were no artificial barriers, no hands waiting to catch me. Just an open world full of triggers and the raw, undistracted truth. The walls I once relied on to hold me up were gone. I had to stand on my own, or I would fall for good.

The battle wasn't just in my body—it was in my mind. The craving was a voice, and it didn't yell. It knew how to get to me, how to twist my thoughts into something that made sense in the moment. *You can't do this alone. Just one hit to take the edge off. You know I'm here for you.* I needed to find a way to tell that voice to shut the fuck up.

I squeezed my eyes shut, grinding my teeth. It was relentless. I had drowned in this voice before, convincing myself that the pain and the shame would be lighter if I just silenced them for a little while. But a little while was never just that.

This wasn't just about stopping. It was about changing everything I had built my life around: the chase, the high, the escape. I had measured time by the space between fixes and structured my days around getting, using, and recovering. Now I had to relearn how to just exist.

Panic clawed at me. My mind scrambled for an escape route. *How long can I do this? What if I fail again?*

Then another thought surfaced. *What if I don't?*

That thought hit differently. It wasn't some forced positive affirmation or a promise. It was a possibility. And this time that possibility felt real.

The temptation slithered through my thoughts, repeating over and over, just one more hit. But I knew the truth. One would never be enough. It never was. I needed to own this shit.

No walls, no staff, just raw willpower and the desperate need to prove to myself that I could. My legs shook, but I didn't collapse. I stood. And finally, in what felt like forever, I recognized the Jonathan who refused to quit. This was the moment I knew—I had the belief, the courage, and the strength. If I could hold on to him—fight for him—then maybe, for the first time, I was truly free.

After 1,592 days—227 weeks, 52 months—I finally did what I once thought was impossible—I let go. I wasn't going back—not now, not ever!

25

THE PAIN OF CLARITY

Clarity doesn't come softly—it cuts. The moment I saw things clearly, I felt the weight of everything I had lost and everything I would have to leave behind. There is something about standing at the bottom again. No title. No status. No direction. No blueprint for what came next. No clear path, only the weight of past decisions and the uncertainty of what came next. No fallback, just me, standing at ground zero, realizing that if I wanted anything, I had to build it myself. No sense of who you are or where you're going. Just the raw, unfiltered truth you have to build. And that was where I was.

I had fought my way out of addiction, but now I had no idea what came next. I was twenty-four, but it felt like I was eighteen all over again, except this time there were no excuses and no running from reality. I wasn't just trying to stay sober; I was trying to exist in a world that had moved on without me. I had spent years numbing, escaping, surviving. But what happens when the fight is over? That's when the grind began.

When I hit thirty days sober, I wasn't proud—I was doing the same thing I'd done since I was ten, just surviving. My body still ached, my mind still waged war with itself, and every part of me wanted to give in.

At sixty days I caught my reflection in the mirror and saw someone I didn't recognize. My face had filled out, my eyes had cleared, but the man staring back at me still resembled a bum.

Ninety days in, the cravings weren't just quieter; they were losing their grip on me, but the fear of relapse sat heavy in my chest.

At six months, the fear of relapse didn't control me anymore, but clarity did—and clarity came with its own price. The more I saw things for what they were, the harder they were to carry. The weight of everything I had lost, everything I wanted, and everything I was still too afraid to face became impossible to ignore.

Then came one year. When that day arrived, I cried, just like I had during the worst of my withdrawals. But these tears weren't the same. They weren't about pain; they were about survival. I had done something I once believed impossible. I wasn't just sober; I was free.

THE WORK BEFORE THE WORK

The jobs came first. Not passion. Not purpose. Just survival. I took whatever work I could find—3:00 a.m. alarms, 4:00 a.m. shifts. Target's warehouse was cold, the cement floor unforgiving. I unloaded fifty-foot shipping containers by hand, one box at a time. By 6:00 a.m., when the trucks were empty, I was tagging clothes, the plastic snapping between my fingers, my mind detached from my body. Wayne, my best friend, who had pulled some strings to get me hired, walked by one morning. He took one look at my face and laughed. "This ain't it, huh?" And he was right. But I didn't have the luxury of quitting.

Hitachi Automotive wasn't much better. By the end of my ten-hour shift, my hands were black with grease, my nose clogged with black snot, my lungs thick with dust, and my back screaming from lifting alternators that would never carry my name. I could disassemble hundreds of them, but I couldn't build a single one if I tried.

It was a relentless grind. A place where time stretched, where ambition suffocated, where the best part of the day was the moment you left.

Of all the dead-end jobs I took, Frederick's of Hollywood was, without a doubt, the most . . . stimulating. After endless shifts unloading boxes at Target and inhaling dust at Hitachi, here I was, handling lace, latex, and battery-powered surprises. It wasn't exactly my life's purpose, but I did learn an important life lesson: Always check if the batteries are included.

Through all these journeys, it was still better than the life I had before because every day I clocked in, I was proving to myself that I could function again. That I could show up. That I could endure. And I knew I'd regret it if I didn't.

THE WEIGHT I COULDN'T CARRY

The jobs were supposed to keep me too busy to think. But clarity doesn't let you hide. No matter how many shifts I worked, no matter how exhausted I was at the end of the day, the truth always found me in the quiet moments. The spaces between the grind, that was when the miscarriages and stillbirth hit me. I had spent years fighting to rebuild, but some things you can't rebuild. Some things are just gone. And in that loss, I realized what I wanted more than anything. Children.

And that was when the next war started. Not the war of survival. The war of choice. Because how do you walk away from someone who stood by you during the worst part of your life? How do you leave when you've been so dependent? How do you leave with integrity? How do you leave when you know people will hate you for it? "She stood by him, and what did she get? He left her to have a baby." I heard it before anyone even said it. The whispers, the judgment, the resentment. And it made me hesitate.

THE CONVERSATION

I turned to my father, Pastor Jonas Crawford. Yes, four wives, seven kids, and now a man of God. If he could change, so could I.

I laid it all out—the guilt, the fear, the weight of staying and leaving.

He didn't hesitate. "Boy," he said, shaking his head, "I didn't give your marriage one year, but here you are at ten. And I knew one day this would happen." Then he leaned forward. "You need to ask yourself if you can go a lifetime without ever having kids and have no regret. Whatever that answer is, it will guide you." He wasn't telling me what to do. He was just forcing me to face the answer I already knew.

THE CHOICE NO ONE WANTS TO MAKE

Telling Melissa was one of the hardest things I ever had to do. I had played the conversation over in my head for a year, imagining every possible reaction—anger, resentment, maybe even relief. But when I finally sat her down, my voice nearly cracked under the weight of what I was about to say. "I need to talk to you about something," I started, my palms damp with sweat. "I've been thinking about this for a long time, and I need to be honest with you. I want children, and I don't think I can go my whole life without having my own." Melissa didn't say anything at first. She just looked at me, searching my face for something. And then she exhaled, nodding slowly. "I knew this day would come," she said. "I knew it on our wedding day."

Her voice wasn't bitter; it was understanding, and that made the pain hurt even more. She had always known I was meant to go out into the world and do great things, even when I didn't. And now I was asking her to let go. I told her that I wasn't walking away from everything we had built and the connection we shared. That I still cared. That I didn't want to hurt her, even though I knew I already had. She wiped a tear from her cheek and gave me a sad smile. "I just hope you find what you're looking for and that God blesses you with a child that I can meet one day." But the hardest conversation wasn't with Melissa. It was with my stepson.

THE FAMILY

When I sat down with my stepson to tell him I was leaving, I expected anger, maybe even resentment. I had prepared myself for that. What I hadn't prepared for was his tears. "What about our family?" he asked. "What about the grandkids?" He was married with two daughters at the time. I had been there for birthdays, for scraped knees, for lessons on how to show up. And now in his eyes, I was leaving. Not just Melissa but also *them*.

I swallowed the lump in my throat. "Nothing changes," I told him. "I am still Pops. I am still Pepa. I will always be here for you, for the girls, as long as you allow me to. This isn't me walking away from you. It's me walking toward something I know I need." But what I never shared was that I was frightened at the thought of losing them. I needed them in my life more than ever. I had experienced enough loss. But standing there, seeing the pain in his eyes, I wondered if this was a new kind of loss—one that I chose. Was I breaking something that could never be rebuilt?

Tears ran down our faces. I opened my arms to hug him, holding on to him as if reassuring both of us that we would be okay. Clarity had robbed me of the comfort of believing everything would be okay. I was making the right choice. I knew that. But knowing doesn't stop it from hurting. Family isn't determined by blood—it's proven in the moments where loyalty, love, and commitment outlast circumstance and the promises we keep even when everything else changes.

I was standing at the edge of regret, staring at both paths—one where I stayed out of my vows and guilt and one where I chose the life I knew I wanted. Melissa deserved more than a man who stayed just because he was afraid to leave. *But clarity showed me that staying out of guilt would be just as much of a betrayal as leaving.*

But what about my step-kids? They weren't just hers. They were mine. The thought of losing them ripped me apart. But love built outside of obligation has a chance to survive. And I had to believe that.

WHAT I CHOSE TO CARRY

I didn't walk away clean. Regret doesn't disappear just because you make the right choice. The cost of clarity is the weight of knowing exactly what you had to leave behind—and the echoes of what might have been. But I made peace with it.

Decades later, my step-kids still call me "Pops." That title was never just a name—it was a bond, one that no divorce, no distance, no changed circumstance could break. It has been one of the greatest joys of my life to carry that role, to show up in the ways that mattered most. Because through all the changes, through the hurt and the healing, we built something that lasted.

Clarity doesn't make things easier; it makes them unavoidable. But even pain has a purpose, and even loss can lead you where you need to go. The right choice doesn't always feel right at first. But when you build something real from the pieces, you realize breaking wasn't the end. It was the beginning.

If you're ready, write a truth you finally accepted—even though it hurt. Now write what you're doing with that truth today. If the answer is "nothing," decide what your next move is.

26

TAKING FLIGHT

The *Daily Breeze* newspaper was the first job that I interviewed for that really inspired me. It represented the first real opportunity outside of warehousing and gave me hope for something bigger. The role focused on sales, specifically classified and display ads. During the interview, they expressed interest in hiring me—if I could pass a typing test. Despite having learned to type in high school, my skills were rusty. I failed the first attempt, managing only seventeen words per minute against the requirement of thirty-five. Determined, I practiced in libraries every day, but nerves got the better of me on the retest, where I scored thirty-three words per minute.

I'd been on plenty of interviews and faced my fair share of disappointments, but this one stung differently. I left heartbroken, but it also lit a fire. Shortly after, I landed a permanent job with a copier manufacturer, performing inside sales and customer service. Within four months I was promoted, only to be laid off after a company event. The cycle of highs and lows was exhausting, but it continued to build my resilience.

A silver lining appeared when a former colleague, now working as a recruiter for an employment agency, reached out. She remembered my work ethic and professionalism and offered to help me find a role. My confidence was fragile, but I knew I couldn't go back to warehouse work, so I filled out the application and hoped for the best.

A few weeks later, I received a call from my contact about a job opportunity at Keystone Communications, a teleport service provider. A teleport is a ground-based communication hub that serves as the nerve center for broadcast transmissions. Equipped with satellite dishes, antennas, and advanced technology, it sends and receives audio, video, and data signals across vast distances. Acting as a gateway, the teleport seamlessly relays live and on-demand content via satellite, fiber optics, or radio frequencies to audiences worldwide. This enables real-time connectivity for broadcasters, internet providers, and global enterprises.

They described it as a fast-paced, high-pressure environment like working in a newsroom. The job was temporary to permanent, paid $10.50 per hour, and came with a warning: Many temps didn't last a week. The thirty-mile commute in LA traffic would be daunting, but I had no other options on the table. After a three-part interview, I got the call—and accepted the position while standing in a phone booth. I had no idea what I was stepping into, but I decided to take the leap.

ENTERING THE UNKNOWN

I started as a traffic coordinator, essentially the air traffic control of broadcasting. My job was to coordinate live broadcast transmissions, ensuring every antenna, satellite, and fiber connection worked seamlessly. It was a technical, high-stakes environment, but I loved the challenge. Every broadcast depended on precision—there was no room for error. From Madison Square Garden events to breaking news across the globe, I was part of making it all happen.

Day 1 was overwhelming. They walked me through the basics of satellite connectivity with diagrams and technical jargon that sounded like another language. My initial reaction? Panic. But as they explained how everything worked, I found myself intrigued. It wasn't just a job; it was a puzzle, and I wanted to figure it out.

But there was another layer to my apprehension that I couldn't ignore. Beneath the surface, I wrestled with a gnawing sense of impostor syndrome. How could someone like me, with a rocky past and no technical experience, belong in a role like this? I couldn't shake the fear that at any moment, someone might discover I wasn't good enough or didn't belong. What if they judged me for my past or saw through the confidence I was struggling to project? This was a dream opportunity, and I couldn't let myself ruin it. The stakes felt enormous, not just professionally but also personally. For the first time in years, a door had opened, and I couldn't let my own self-doubt close it.

As I settled into the role, I started to compartmentalize my life, putting up a barrier between my professional and personal worlds. I created two separate identities, ensuring they would never intersect. This was also a way to avoid my past because the fear and vulnerability were enormous. I could have minimized the self-doubt had I realized that the transformations I had already undergone were precisely the reason I was able to create this opportunity for myself in the first place.

The learning curve was steep, but I had a mentor who made sure I kept up. My boss—nicknamed "the Colonel" for her rigorous standards—pushed me hard. She expected excellence and didn't accept excuses, but she also made sure I was prepared. By week 3, I was thrown into the deep end. Left alone while others stepped away, I answered a client call—something I technically wasn't supposed to do yet—and handled the request successfully. That moment changed everything. When my boss returned, she reviewed my work and decided I was ready for more responsibilities.

BUILDING CONFIDENCE

Within sixty days, Keystone hired me permanently, recognizing my growth and initiative. The commute was brutal—an hour and a half each way—but I established a routine. Waking up at 4:00 a.m., leaving by 4:45 a.m., and returning home around 8:00 p.m. became my norm. This structure gave me stability during a time of personal challenges and reinforced discipline in my life. The job wasn't just a paycheck; it became a lifeline.

Still, there were days when fear crept in, whispering doubts. I'd catch myself wondering, *What if I mess up? What if they see through me?* There was a constant battle to quiet those thoughts and remind myself that I was capable. I couldn't afford to let fear of judgment or failure sabotage what I had built. This role wasn't just a chance to grow professionally—it was a chance to prove to myself that I could rise above my past.

But there was an additional fear—a deeper one I barely wanted to acknowledge. The last time my life felt like it was on an upward trajectory, it all ended abruptly with the death of my sister. I'd experienced joy and success before, only to have it ripped away. What if history repeated itself? What if this new chapter, this fragile ray of sunshine, was destined to fade like the last one? The thought of losing everything again weighed heavily on my heart, though I tried to bury it beneath the routine and discipline that kept me moving forward.

Over the next seven months, I built a reputation for going beyond the call of duty. I worked every holiday, took on extra shifts, and learned every detail of my role. When a supervisor position opened, I hesitated to apply. My initial reaction was to make excuses. I didn't want to give up my weekday morning shift to work weekends and swing shifts. I convinced myself that others were more qualified, that I hadn't been with the company long enough, and that someone with a better background deserved the role. These thoughts felt safe—they kept me in my *growth cage*.

When my supervisor confronted me about my reluctance, she said something that hit me hard: "I cannot believe you will pass up an opportunity for growth because of your work hours." I felt so small because of my weak-ass excuses. She continued, "I don't want you to think I'm picking on you by giving you more work. I see something in you, so I have been preparing you to be able to take my job one day." My thoughts were confined by the boundaries I'd placed around myself to protect my comfort zone, my imposter syndrome, and the other two controlling my life—*self-doubt and self-sabotage*. The fear of exposing my vulnerability had taken over. I was caught in a battle between my mind saying, "No way," and my heart whispering, "You can do this."

Despite the fear, I applied. Initially, I didn't get the job. While disappointed, I was acknowledged with a letter of accommodation, a raise, and a gift card. The very next day, the general manager called me into her office and offered me the position after all. That reversal was a turning point. It taught me that risks can pay off and that I was capable of more than I gave myself credit for.

THE COST OF COMFORT

Staying in my comfort zone felt safe, but it came with a steep price. Every time I clung to familiar routines or avoided stepping into unfamiliar territory, I sacrificed opportunities for growth. Comfort wasn't just limiting—it was suffocating. To grow, I had to embrace discomfort, taking risks that felt daunting but necessary. Each step into the unknown revealed strength and capability I didn't know I had. The cost of staying comfortable was stagnation, and I couldn't afford to pay it any longer.

THE WEIGHT OF WHAT-IFS

With every challenge came a barrage of "what-ifs." What if I wasn't ready? What if I failed? What if I let everyone down? These questions didn't just linger—they felt like anchors, pulling at my confidence. But as I moved forward, I realized there was a heavier burden: What if I never tried? What if I let fear stop me from discovering my potential? Leaning into those doubts didn't erase them, but each success made their weight lighter, day by day.

FROM EXCUSES TO EXECUTION

Excuses were easy. They offered an escape—a way to avoid failure, embarrassment, or discomfort. But excuses weren't what this role demanded. Each day brought new challenges, and hesitation wasn't an option. The voice of self-doubt still lingered, but I silenced it with action. Every task completed, every risk taken proved that I was capable. Moving from excuses to execution didn't just change how I worked—it reshaped the person I was daring to become.

My journey from a temporary to permanent employee, and eventually to leadership, wasn't just professional growth; *it was the possibilities I allowed myself to imagine and the start of believing in my own potential.* And this time I refused to let anyone, including myself, dim *the light of possibility.*

27

FUCK!

Fuck comfort. Fuck stability. Fuck stagnation. Fuck waiting for the perfect moment. If you don't disrupt your own life, life will do it for you—and trust me, it won't be fucking gentle. I learned that the hard way when I unwrapped a train set that wrecked me in ways I never saw coming.

It was Christmas. Melissa and my stepdaughter handed me a gift, wrapped neatly, just like any other present. But when I tore back the paper and saw what was inside, everything stopped. A train set. A simple, harmless fucking train set. But to me, it was twenty-three years of fucking silence finally breaking me open.

I gripped the box, my hands tightening around it. Suddenly, I was ten years old again, sitting cross-legged on the floor, watching my five-year-old brother tear into the wrapping paper of a train set I had wanted years before he was born but never received. I sat there, swallowing the hurt, telling myself it didn't matter. But it did. And now here it was again, staring me in the face. It wasn't just an old wish resurfacing—it was a gut punch from my past, forcing me to reckon with emotions I thought I had outgrown.

Before I could stop it, the tears came. Deep, gasping, body-shaking tears. The kind that doesn't just come from sadness but from the weight of years pressing down all at once. My twenty-one-year-old stepdaughter looked at me, completely confused. "Pops, it's just a train set." But that wasn't just a train. It was the fucking disruption I needed to break the pain of my lost childhood.

Melissa knew this story. I had shared it with her before—how much that train meant to me as a kid, how I had swallowed the disappointment, convincing myself it didn't matter. And here she was, a year after our split, handing me a piece of my childhood back. We laughed later, joking that it was a good thing she waited because if she had given it to me years earlier, I probably would have sold it for drug money.

But that train did something more than just bring back a memory. It sparked something. It made me think about all the things little John-John had wanted, all the dreams and small joys I had dismissed. And from that day forward, I started buying all kinds of toys, knocking out a bucket list of sorts—the things that little boy had once dreamed of but never got. And sure, I could have bought myself a train set a hundred times before. But it wouldn't have hit the same. It wouldn't have been the disruption I needed.

Sometimes the disruptions we need the most are the ones we never see coming. Some hit like a wrecking ball, uninvited and unwanted. Looking back, some of my biggest breakthroughs came from the disruptions I swore would break me. What I thought was an ending was just a *demolition before the rebuild.*

FUCK SURVIVAL MODE

Survival is the starting line, not the finish line. We romanticize survival. We wear it like a badge of honor. "I survived." But here's the thing: *Survival isn't success. It's just not dying.* For years I had built an identity around being the guy who made it through—the comeback story. And the problem with that? It meant I always had to be coming back from something. I didn't know how to exist outside the struggle.

The thing about survival mode is that it's exhausting. It keeps you on high alert, always waiting for the next hit, the next loss, the next thing to push through. I had survived so much, but I wasn't living. I was just bracing for impact. And the worst part? I had convinced myself that was the smart thing to do. That staying ready for disappointment meant I wouldn't be caught off guard. But what it really meant was that I was never truly present, never fully allowing myself to experience trust, success, or even joy. And that's no way to build a future. *The real cost of survival mode isn't just exhaustion—it's isolation. You build walls so high that even the right people can't get through.* You convince yourself that keeping distance is safer, but all it does is keep you stuck. At some point you must ask yourself, "Am I protecting myself, or am I just keeping myself alone?"

I could no longer *glorify survival.* Survival mode is sneaky. It had rewired my mind to trust nothing and no one. Because when you live in survival mode for too long, trusting people feels like an unnecessary risk. You question motives, expect betrayal, and struggle to believe that stability is real. So I say fuck survival mode! Set yourself free.

FUCK EXPECTATION AND VALIDATION

I had spent my whole life meeting expectations—mine, my family's, society's. Be strong. Keep moving. Don't fail. But no one ever tells you that expectations can be another form of survival.

I wasn't living for myself. I was living for the image of who I thought I was supposed to be. And coming out of addiction and navigating my way back into the world made it even harder. I had rebuilt so much of my life, but I was still learning how to manage the weight of expectations, both old and new. My empathy had grown, my understanding of struggle had deepened, and with that, my instinct to say yes never faded. But I had to learn that saying yes didn't have to mean losing myself. It could mean choosing who and what I gave my energy to, not out of obligation but out of intention.

I no longer needed fucking validation to confirm my growth. But there was one place I kept looking for it—one person I kept hoping would give me the words I never heard: my mother. When I reminded her of her response to my molestation, she acted like she had forgotten. Like it wasn't as bad as I remembered. Like it wasn't something I should still be carrying. I was still searching for that hug, for those words—"I'm sorry this happened to you." But they never came. Only defensiveness. Only "I did the best I could." And honestly? I believe that. I do. But that didn't change the fact that I was still waiting for something that would never come. And at that moment I knew that it was time to let go of the fucking validation I had been chasing my entire life.

I had nothing to prove. My success, my resilience, my ability to rebuild—none of it required permission or applause. Validation had been a survival tool, a way to measure my worth in the eyes of others. But now? Now I was learning that true freedom came from knowing I was enough without external approval. And the more I played the role, the more I lost sight of who the fuck I was.

WHO THE FUCK AM I?

For the first time, I had no one to answer to but myself, no one to shape my decisions, and no safety net to fall back on. Just me. And I was fucking scared.

Living on my own now was nothing like when I was homeless, sleeping in my car. That was about survival, just making it to the next day. But now I had an apartment—four walls and a door that locked. Stability, at least on the surface. But that first night? It was scary, exhilarating, and lonely all at once. The silence was loud. No chaos to fight through, no distractions. Just me. And the reason I knew this time in my life was necessary? Because I needed to finally face myself. I needed to discover who the fuck I really was—beyond the boy, the son, the brother, the husband, the stepfather, the addict, and the survivor.

Still carrying my father wound, I had spent my whole life moving from one dependency to another. First, my mom's house until age twenty. Then straight into marriage, which gave me security in ways I didn't fully understand at the time. Let's be real—there was no way I could have been on my own financially at twenty. I felt like I could "man up" in the role of husband, but the truth was, I leaned on that stability far more than I was willing to admit. I wasn't just building a marriage; I was holding on to a lifeline. I had learned to shape myself based on what was needed in the moment, but the truth was, I had never really learned how to exist on my own terms. My sense of worth had always been tied to proving something—proving I could bounce back, proving I could be needed, proving I could be someone worth keeping around. But at what point did I stop proving and start living for myself? Still seeking some form of grounding outside of myself. But who the fuck was I when all that was stripped away?

Every version of me had been created in response to the world around me, built out of necessity rather than choice. Jonathan was the professional who strategized, adapted, and made moves. JoNathan (pronounced Joe-Nathan) was the tough country boy born in the city, the one who loved his cowboy boots since age thirteen. JC was the cool one, the guy who projected confidence even when he was uncertain.

All my life I had switched between them, playing the role required for the moment. But now I had to ask, "Who the fuck am I outside of survival mode?" It was time to disrupt these fucking singular personalities and merge them into one authentic person. For the first time, I didn't have to switch between identities to fit the moment. I could be all of them, or none of them, because I started to see who I was outside of survival. That realization? It was both terrifying and freeing.

FUCK FEAR

Fear doesn't just stop you from taking risks—it convinces you that staying put is the safest option. *Fear whispers that stability, even when unfulfilling, is better than uncertainty.* It tricks you into believing that the struggle you know is better than the success you don't.

I thought fear only existed in failure. But I learned that fear shows up in success too. Fear of stepping into something new. Fear keeps you locked in cycles disguised as stability. But the truth is, *fear doesn't give a shit about you. Fear doesn't protect you. It keeps you in your place—small.*

Fucking fear means calling it out for what it is. It means refusing to let the unknown hold you hostage. It means stepping forward even when every part of you wants to stay where it's comfortable. *Because comfort is the enemy of growth, and fear is the anchor that keeps you stuck.* Comfort zones are just waiting rooms for regret. And I refuse to sit in one.

So fuck fear. Fuck the need for certainty. Fuck the excuses. Fear will always be there, but you get to decide if it controls you, fuels you, or fucks you!

FUCKING LIFE UP WITH PURPOSE

When you combine fucking disruption with fucking purpose, oh, you have fire. You have momentum. You have something unstoppable. Disruption by itself shakes things up, but purpose? Purpose gives it direction. Purpose makes the chaos meaningful. It turns destruction into reinvention, struggle into strategy.

Disruption without purpose is the cost of growth. But when you add intention to it, that's where the real shit happens. That's where you stop waiting and start choosing. That's when fucking your life up stops being about breaking things and starts being about fucking building the life you want.

Disruption will come whether you're ready or not. The difference is in how you handle it. If you're stuck, disrupt the routine that's keeping you there. If you're waiting for permission, disrupt the need to be validated. If you're afraid of failure, disrupt the belief that failure is the worst thing that can happen. (Hint: Staying the same is worse.) *Disruption isn't the enemy; complacency is.*

WHAT'S FUCKING YOU UP RIGHT NOW?

So now I ask you—what's your train set? Maybe it's time to unwrap your own disruption. What the fuck do you need to let go of? What's the thing that you tell yourself doesn't matter, but deep down you know it does? What's the moment you've been avoiding? What belief is keeping you small? What fucking excuses are you still holding on to? What version of yourself are you refusing to release because it's comfortable? Disruption with purpose isn't chaos. It's clarity. It's courage. Because disruption isn't about destruction; it's about evolution. The ones who wield disruption with purpose are the ones who shape the game.

Are you fucking up your own limits or letting them fuck you up? Because if you're letting them fuck you up, then you're fucked!

This is a must: Make your own "Fuck This!" list—fear, stagnation, self-doubt, needing approval—whatever has been holding you back. Then write one bold sentence that answers, "Who the fuck am I now?" Say it out loud. That's your new standard.

28

THE PRESSURE TO PROVE

One month into my supervisor position, the phone rang at 1:30 a.m. Eastern Daylight Time, shattering the silence of my swing shift. "There's been a bombing at the Olympics!" My pulse accelerated as I pieced together the implications: chaos, panic, and a logistical nightmare for our satellite transmissions, *the process of sending broadcast signals from one location to multiple location simultaneously.* It was the kind of test you can't prepare for, but somehow I knew this was a defining moment—not just for the company but also for me. Would I step up or step back?

On the night of July 27, 1996, the Summer Olympics in Atlanta, Georgia, became the epicenter of a national tragedy. The bombing in Centennial Olympic Park, a hub of celebration and unity, left two dead and over a hundred injured. The ripple effects were immediate. Our company was responsible for transmitting the main broadcast for the rights holders of the 1996 Olympic Games, making us a critical link in delivering the event to the world. When the bombing occurred, it disrupted our ability to transmit, plunging operations into chaos. My task was clear: work with our network operations team to restore service as quickly as possible. Broadcasting outages, damaged circuits, and panic behind the scenes painted a stark picture of just how fragile even the most robust systems could be under extreme distress. I led our response, balancing the need for speed with the urgency of accuracy. The experience was a trial by fire, but it taught me that resilience doesn't mean perfection—it means adaptability in the face of the unknown. It was my first professional test of proving I could handle extreme pressure, and it would not be my last. *Pressure doesn't create cracks; it reveals character.*

Months later I faced another pivotal moment, tasked with optimizing our satellite inventories to generate much-needed revenue for the company. This wasn't just about logistics; it was about proving myself before a managerial restructuring—and battling the fear that said, "What if you're not good enough?" Each spreadsheet and sleepless night became a silent battlefield where I fought against my own doubts, pushing myself to show I could deliver tangible results.

Fear has a way of amplifying doubt, but it also sharpens focus. I spent weeks agonizing over how to approach the task, unsure if I could deliver. One morning, as I stared at another blank spreadsheet, I had a revelation: The key lay in the early hours when satellite usage was minimal. By reallocating resources and outsourcing lower-revenue services to third parties, I created new blocks of airtime to sell during peak hours. The plan worked, and within months the company started seeing higher revenues. This achievement wasn't just a line on my résumé; it was the deliberate construction of self-esteem and capability that I was building brick by brick. *Transformation begins the moment you stop fearing failure and start seeing opportunity.*

But not every moment was a victory. Early on I misjudged the timing of a pay raise request. My eagerness clashed with my boss's expectations, serving as a humbling reminder that strategy isn't just about execution but also about patience and foresight. I wanted a raise. It was the first time I'd ever had a job with real potential to earn more, and I was riding a wave of mental momentum. I felt unstoppable, reaching for the sky. But along with that excitement came vulnerability—I was terrified of hearing the word "no."

In hindsight, my timing couldn't have been worse. The company had just been acquired by France Telecom and rebranded as Globecast North America. With the acquisition came a new chain of command, including a brand-new boss. While he'd heard great things about me and seen my performance on paper, the truth was he didn't know me. And in a newly merged environment, paper résumés don't carry the same weight as personal trust. He hadn't witnessed my skills in action or had time to build a real connection, but I felt the raise was warranted because I had been in my role for a year and exceeded expectations. I had a sense of entitlement, not realizing he needed time to get settled, learn the team, and make informed decisions about the department.

When the answer came back as no, it stung. I felt like I had overreached or misjudged the moment. But to his credit, my boss handled it with grace—offering understanding, empathy, and a clear path forward. What I didn't realize at the time was that this defining moment would shape my own leadership style. His approach to rejection would become a lesson I'd mirror as I grew into my own leadership journey. Perhaps the most important takeaway was to never stop creating value. That mindset became the cornerstone of my success. Rejection didn't stop me—it sharpened me. It taught me patience, persistence, and the power of continually proving my self-worth.

In 1998 I became the satellite resources supervisor, and a major satellite operator, PanAmSat, suffered a catastrophic failure on the Galaxy 4 satellite. This failure created ripple effects across the country, halting operations for critical services such as paging systems for doctors and television programming for networks such as UPN, Paramount, and Sony Studios. It was in this chaotic environment that I was tasked with finding solutions to help our clients mitigate the impact on their operations. The magnitude of the failure was staggering, and with limited resources at the company's disposal, I had just three days to stabilize operations. This outage was more than a technical issue—it became a test of my skills, my preparedness, and frankly, whether I really knew my shit.

This situation also brought out the worst in my internal dialogue. The conversations between me, myself, and I intensified: "Can you do this? How the hell will you get through this one? Why can't you just keep shit simple?" *Doubt is the loudest voice when you're on the brink of something great.* But there was no time for doubt to linger. The company's future was at stake, and I had to push all that noise aside. Instead of spiraling out of control, I stepped into the moment with clarity, calmness, and the readiness to lead.

The temporary solution I devised by the early morning hours minimized service disruptions for critical operations. By prioritizing bandwidth for our clients' most urgent needs and reallocating resources across lower-priority systems, I managed to stabilize key services. But the work wasn't done. Over the following days, I collaborated with engineers and suppliers to develop a longer-term strategy focused on creating efficiencies and increasing utilization with the limited resources we had. This approach saved the company $2 million in costs that year and $1 million annually over the next three years. This dual approach, addressing immediate needs while planning for sustainable improvements, further demonstrated my ability to lead. Within six months this crisis had an unexpected upside: My boss, having witnessed my leadership, secured a 10 percent pay increase for me. It was validation that persistence and value creation don't go unnoticed.

The result of these actions led to many achievements. Three years after joining the company, I earned a promotion to manager of satellite resources and cost control, where I was entrusted with ensuring the efficiency and profitability of our satellite operations and managing cost. It wasn't just a step forward in title—it was a shift in how I saw myself and my potential.

In the following two years, I continued to ascend, taking on cross-managerial functions: manager of syndication, manager of sports services, and eventually I was responsible for managing the same department I started in as a temp. Each position challenged me to expand my capabilities, think strategically, and lead with intention. With every new role, I honed my skills and redefined my professional brand, pushing the boundaries of what I thought I could achieve.

These experiences were not merely about financial gain or career advancement—they were about transformation. They taught me the intricacies of leadership, the importance of adaptability, and the necessity of cultivating trust within my teams. I grew not just as a professional but also as a person, learning to navigate high-stakes situations with resilience and clarity.

I began this path weighed down by fear, self-doubt, and a near absence of self-belief. But each step forward challenged me to grow.

Little by little I evolved into a leader with vision, confidence, and the resolve to tackle whatever came my way.

This wasn't the conclusion of my story—it was the prologue to a new chapter. Every success introduced fresh challenges, higher expectations, and invaluable lessons. I came to understand that proving myself wasn't a single milestone. It wasn't something you check off and move past. It was a continuous process—a relentless pursuit to rise to every occasion, meet every challenge, and demonstrate my worth time and again.

This realization prepared me for what lay ahead. Pivotal moments awaited me, moments that would demand resilience, sharp strategic thinking, and an unwavering belief in my ability to persevere. These trials became the foundation of what I now call *the Pressure to Prove*—an ethos that has guided me through every challenge and breakthrough.

As I reflect on this journey, I see how these moments shaped more than my career—they transformed how I lead, how I grow, and how I embrace challenges.

PART IV

RISE—NO APOLOGIES. NO MASK. JUST RISE.

Growth hurts too—but at least it
gets you somewhere.

29

THE WEIGHT OF GROWTH

The email landed with a thud in my inbox: a $3 million discrepancy discovered ahead of an audit, and the task of finding it had my name all over it. No pressure, right? The weight of the task wasn't just in the numbers; it was the unspoken message: "Oh shit, can you handle this?" It was a challenge, an opportunity to prove that my role wasn't just about showing up but stepping up. *Growth rarely announces itself—it arrives disguised as a challenge that makes you question everything you thought you were capable of.*

I had never flown on an airplane before, and now at thirty-four I was ordered to be in Miami by Monday morning to "find that damn money"—the CEO's words, not mine. As we sped down the runway, my heart was racing, and I was gripping the armrest like it owed me money. As the plane lifted off, I silently wondered if I should've written a will or at least called my mom one more time. But as we leveled out and I realized I wasn't plummeting to my death, I started to relax—just a little.

That was when it hit me. Growing up, my world felt trapped by the chaos of gang-infested neighborhoods and the invisible walls of the state line. There were no guards, checkpoints, or barriers keeping me in, but the absence of opportunity, the weight of fear, and the pull of survival made leaving feel impossible. To me, the world outside wasn't just far away; it felt like a privilege reserved for someone else, not someone like me.

As the plane soared higher, the rumble of takeoff resonated deeply. The pressure of uncovering $3 million was real, but the burdens of my past, addiction, and the constant fight for redemption carried a heavier weight. If I could survive those, surely, I could survive this. That thought carried me through the turbulence, both literal and metaphorical.

DISCOVERY AND REDEMPTION

Arriving in Miami, I was greeted by the sweltering heat and the intimidating reality of working directly under the scrutiny of the CEO and CFO. My boss wasn't there to act as a buffer or a shield. This was my moment, and it was terrifying. Every morning, as I walked into the headquarters, I felt the weight of my fears pressing on me. Would today be the day I failed? Would I miss something? Would my findings fall apart under their scrutiny? *Some challenges don't just test your skills; they test your resolve to show up every day, even when fear whispers that you won't succeed.*

The CEO and CFO were sharp, seasoned, and direct. They asked tough questions and expected precise answers. Each day felt like a marathon of stress and self-doubt, but I kept going. Somewhere in the depths of my mind, I kept reminding myself, "You've survived worse than this."

After my first grueling twelve-hour day, I remember walking into the hotel, passing the bar on my way to my room. For the first time in years, I had a real craving for a stiff drink. The stress of the day had been unrelenting. But what good would it do me? Tomorrow would bring another long day of digging through data, spreadsheets, and printouts, so I knew that I would need every ounce of energy and clarity I could muster, something a hangover and a foggy mind couldn't provide me. The decision not to indulge was more than just practical; it was a moment of growth, a choice to stay aligned with the person I was striving to become.

Finally, the breakthrough came. Costs had been allocated to resources and service orders that had never been invoiced, leading to years of lost revenue and accrued cost. Presenting my findings to the executive team was like walking into a courtroom, the air heavy with expectation. I laid out the numbers, the errors, and the solution. Silence followed, then a single nod from the CEO. It wasn't just a nod of approval; it was a nod that said, "You bring value."

That moment marked a shift. It wasn't just a win for the company; it was a win for me. It was proof to myself that I could carry the weight of responsibility, that my work mattered, and that I was capable of more than I'd ever imagined. The $3 million saved wasn't just a line item; it was a validation of my journey.

TRANSITIONS AND RESPONSIBILITIES

Leadership is rarely clean or easy. It's shaped in the moments when personal history collides with professional responsibility, when the weight of relationships and decisions forces you to balance empathy with accountability. These are the moments that stretch you, reveal your growth potential, and teach you to lead.

Transitioning into leadership isn't just a promotion; it's a shift in identity. Suddenly, you're no longer "one of the team"; you're the person they look to for answers and direction. One of the toughest parts of that transition was navigating the changing dynamics of relationships. Friends who once laughed with me during breaks now hesitated to share openly, unsure where the boundaries of friendship and authority lay. One moment I was laughing with them about our favorite TV shows, and the next I was sitting across from them in meetings, delivering performance reviews.

The hardest moments came when I had to hold those same friends accountable. One such moment was the day I had to write up a close friend for repeated mistakes that were affecting the company. I remember sitting across from them, feeling the tension between us. “This isn't personal,” I said, though I knew it would feel that way. By the time the meeting ended, so had the friendship. The employee avoided interaction after that—no more handshakes or conversations—and it made me question whether it had ever been a true friendship in the first place.

That day I learned a hard truth about leadership: It's not about doing what's easy or popular; it's about doing what's necessary, even when it costs you personally.

It wasn't just peers I had to hold accountable. There came a time when I had to write up two supervisors and terminate an employee with fifteen years of tenure all within one week. Some of these employees I had worked closely with since my days as a temp. Another tough decision came when I had to lay off my cost control team because their job functions were transitioned to headquarters. The average tenure of these employees was ten years, and many had families depending on their income. Sitting across from them during those conversations, I thought of all the times I had been terminated. I remembered how it felt—the uncertainty, the loss, the fear of starting over.

The outcomes of these responsibilities were twofold. My skin grew thicker to handle the weight of these moments, but my heart never stopped caring. I made it a priority to handle every difficult situation with empathy, even when reprimand was extremely justified or when I was angry. Leadership required me to separate my emotions from the responsibility at hand and ensure that fairness and respect guided every decision. Even when decisions were out of my control, I knew how I delivered the message mattered. I couldn't change the outcome, but I could respect the humanity of the people on the receiving end.

Not everyone embraced my transition into leadership. Some questioned my qualifications, while others resisted the changes I tried to implement. Their doubts often mirrored my own. Was I making the right decisions? Did I have what it took to lead? I quickly realized that leadership wasn't about having all the answers. It was about trusting the process and letting failure become a source of power, not a weight against me.

The balancing act of leadership didn't just involve navigating relationships. It also came with the pressure of juggling old responsibilities while taking on new ones. Transitioning to supervisor felt like wearing two hats at once, still managing day-to-day operations while carrying the weight of decisions that affected my teams. Delegation didn't come naturally to me. As a hands-on person, being deeply involved was how I learned and stayed connected to the work. But as I transitioned into leadership, I realized that trying to do everything alone wasn't sustainable.

THE WEIGHT THAT SHAPES US

Leadership arrives with weight—the weight of decisions that ripple far beyond the moment they're made and the weight of growth that pushes you into spaces you never thought you'd occupy. It's not a weight you're ever fully prepared for, but it's one you learn to carry as you grow.

The weight of leadership comes not just from the responsibility but also from the complexity. Every decision you make isn't just about numbers or results; it's also about people, trust, relationships, and the delicate balance of knowing when to push and when to hold back. Leadership forces you to navigate the tension between compassion and accountability, between personal feelings and professional standards. It demands that you confront your own fears and blind spots, the insecurities you've hidden from yourself, and the instincts you need to refine.

What I didn't realize at first was how much this weight would shape me—not just as a leader but also as a person. *The weight of leadership doesn't just test your abilities; it reveals your character.* It taught me that self-leadership is the foundation for leading others. Before you can guide anyone else, you have to guide yourself—to show up with integrity, to stay grounded in chaos, and to push forward even when the path feels impossible.

But self-leadership isn't just about discipline or resilience. It's also becoming someone others can depend on because you've learned to rely on yourself; you've become honest with yourself about your shortcomings and have the courage to confront those gaps, no matter how uncomfortable it feels. Growth doesn't come wrapped in comfort—it demands discomfort. It demands failure. It demands that you carry the weight of responsibility, not as a burden but as a force that makes you stronger.

The weight doesn't just test you—it transforms you. It challenges every part of who you are, but it also shapes who you're becoming. Leadership showed me that every decision, every difficult conversation, and every uncertain step wasn't just about the job—it was about becoming the person I needed to be. It taught me that the same principles that guide great leaders—trust, empathy, and accountability—are the ones that build great people.

Carrying the weight of leadership isn't about perfection or control; it's about progress and connection, learning to live in the tension of growth and recognizing that every struggle is shaping you into someone capable of carrying even more. *The weight is heavy because it matters*. And as much as it demands from you, it also gives you something invaluable in return: a deeper understanding of yourself, your purpose, and your capacity to thrive. *To grow into leadership is to grow into yourself.*

A MOMENT OF RECKONING

For years I didn't think much about ceilings; they weren't part of my survival mindset. My focus was on getting through the day, securing the next opportunity, and staying afloat. But there came a time when I realized I wasn't looking up because I had accepted that the ceiling above me was fixed. It wasn't placed there by anyone else; it was one I had built myself, brick by brick, from years of survival, fear, and self-doubt.

This realization hit me during a meeting with senior leadership. As I sat there, surrounded by people making decisions that affected everything I had worked for, I couldn't shake the feeling that I was boxed in—not because I wasn't capable but because I had started to believe that where I was was as far as I could go. The walls I had fought so hard to climb out of—poverty, drugs, homelessness, and self-doubt—had somehow become the ceiling I couldn't see past.

The silent limitations we impose on ourselves are the hardest to break. For me, it wasn't about someone telling me I couldn't achieve more; it was about me asking myself why I hadn't even tried. Was I afraid of failing? Afraid of wanting too much? Or was I still clinging to the mindset that had carried me through my toughest years: "Just survive"? *But survival is only the beginning.* At some point you must ask yourself, "If I'm not just living to survive, what am I living for?"

That moment was my reckoning. I had to confront my own fears and ask why I was holding back. Why was I settling for "good enough"? Breaking through the glass ceiling wasn't about proving anything to anyone else. It meant redefining what I believed was possible for me, admitting that I had outgrown the limits I had once clung to for safety, and realizing that it was okay to want more.

Breaking through that ceiling wasn't easy. It forced me to let go of old beliefs and the stories I had told myself for years—that ambition was risky, that wanting more was selfish, that someone like me, someone who had spent so many years just trying to survive, didn't belong in the rooms where bigger decisions were made. But what I learned is this: *You don't break through a glass ceiling all at once. You crack it piece by piece, with every risk you take, every fear you face, and every step you move toward something bigger than where you are now.*

Looking back, that ceiling wasn't just a barrier; it was a mirror reflecting all the fears, doubts, and insecurities I needed to confront. And piece by piece, as I broke through it, I began to see not just what was on the other side but who I was becoming in the process.

Try this:

Make two lists.

1. What you lost while growing.
2. What you gained because you grew.

Now underline the ones that matter most—and own the trade.

30

RESET TO RISE

After six years and four promotions, I realized the momentum I had built was starting to blur my vision. The pace of success had been exhilarating but blinding. Everything was happening so fast that I couldn't see beyond my current existence. It was as if I had been running at full speed without stopping to check if I was even on the right track. When I stepped back, the noise of my achievements faded, and I began to see what had been hidden in plain sight: my dreams. And my dreams weren't just big—they were audacious, reaching far beyond what I had allowed myself to imagine. But I needed to ensure they were achievable and not just a fairy tale of my imagination.

Every transformation begins with a decision to leave the comfort of what is and step boldly toward what could be. That's where I found myself. Standing at this crossroads, I wasn't just making a career move—I was making a decision that would redefine how I saw myself and what I believed was possible.

Clarity didn't make the road ahead any easier—it only made the stakes higher. Seeing the possibilities was one thing; acting on it was another. My vision demanded bold moves, so I realized that waiting for an opportunity wasn't an option; I had to create one. I reached out to my network, positioning myself not just as a candidate but as a leader ready to drive transformative change. I leaned on my experiences in operations, managing people, and problem-solving to demonstrate the value I could bring. My persistence and preparation finally paid off when I was invited to interview with the SPACECONNECTION for a director of operations role—a position that felt like a natural evolution of my journey.

My first attempt at the position ended with disappointment. Someone else was selected. It was the first position I had applied for and been told no in four years—and that shit hurt. It was humbling, and it ensured I remained grounded in my quest for more. The first denial taught me that setbacks are not roadblocks—they're recalibrations. Each moment of rejection became fuel and reaffirmed my belief that with my resilience I could overcome anything. I took a reset to focus on refining my leadership skills in my current role, dedicating myself to operational enhancements, standardizing standard operating procedures, and tackling the endless human resource and people problems that came my way. The wealth of knowledge I gained during that year prepared me for whatever direction I chose to pursue next.

A year later, when the position with the SPACECONNECTION reopened, I reapplied, reinterviewed, and this time landed the job. It was a testament to persistence and the power of preparation. Submitting a resignation for the first time in my life was an emotional whirlwind. As I stood outside my boss's office, my nerves were a tangled mix of joy and fear, and my mind raced with doubt. Was I making the right decision? Could I truly leave the security of this place that had been my foundation? *Sometimes the only way to discover your potential is to let go of stability.* As I handed over my letter, my palms were clammy, and my voice wavered ever so slightly. I could feel the weight of every decision I had made leading to this moment pressing on my chest.

After my boss picked his chin up off the floor, he offered me advice that would stick with me: "Stay in the director role for at least one year. It will open many doors for you. And who knows? I may have to come to you for a job one day." Then with a wry smile, he made a request: "I know people like you and respect you as a leader, but please don't take my employees with you." I didn't make any promises—after all, the requests to join me had already started coming in.

As I walked out of my boss's office, I realized that this wasn't an end—it was a beginning. Saying goodbye felt like closing a chapter of my life—one filled with triumphs, struggles, and lessons that shaped who I had become.

The transition to my new role as director of operations wasn't without its challenges. While building trust with my team was a priority, an unexpected challenge came from my peers: Other directors within the organization felt threatened by my arrival. This resistance wasn't overt, but it was enough to create delays as I tried to drive progress. It's one thing to encounter resistance from your team; it's another when it comes from leaders at your level. Navigating this tension required a different kind of leadership. *Collaboration wasn't just a strategy; it was a necessity.*

I couldn't approach them the same way I did my team. Instead, I focused on fostering collaboration. I scheduled regular one-on-one meetings with each of them, not to impose my ideas but to listen and find common ground. It was a delicate balancing act—acknowledging their concerns while staying firm on the changes I knew were necessary for the company's growth. I had to demonstrate that my role wasn't about taking control but about creating value that benefited all of us. Over time my results began to speak louder than any resistance.

During my first ninety days, I focused on earning trust rather than asserting authority. I chose not to hide behind a desk or title. Instead, I embedded myself with the operations team, learning their processes, listening to their frustrations, and demonstrating through action that I was there to support and build with them. *People support what they help create.*

The call center itself posed one of the greatest challenges. The transformation wasn't just about processes or operations—it was about people. It proved that even the most entrenched systems could change when leadership met collaboration head-on. The systems were inefficient, the hours of operation didn't align with client needs, and the team was overextended. My first priority was automation, modernizing workflows to reduce errors and improve response times. But modernization was just the start. Meeting client demands required expanding operational hours and increasing staff to handle the workload. This wasn't just a logistical change—it was a cultural shift. Employees who initially resisted the changes soon began to see the value in innovation, and slowly collaboration replaced resistance. By the end of the transformation, the call center wasn't just running efficiently—it had become a model for adaptability and growth.

The transformation didn't just affect operations—it changed me. This role expanded my identity in profound ways. I wasn't just managing systems; I was interfacing with clients, representing the company at a higher level, and becoming a key driver of its success. My travels grew more frequent, and with each meeting I saw how my presence added value. I even started to release my grip on the armrest—literally and figuratively—as I embraced new opportunities with confidence. Letting go of that grip became symbolic of releasing my fear and embracing the journey ahead. The joke I made about holding on to the armrest "like it owed me money" had followed me into this new role, where I could finally laugh at how much my own growth demanded letting go of the unnecessary.

The decision to reset was one of the most pivotal moments of my life. This reset wasn't just my journey—it's a reminder for anyone standing at the edge of uncertainty: leap. The ground may shift beneath you, but the courage to jump is what creates the path forward. Submitting my resignation wasn't just an act of leaving—it was an act of courage, of betting on myself and my ability to rise to the next challenge.

The emotional toll of that moment was heavy because transformation demands discomfort. It asks you to trade certainty for possibility, safety for potential, and familiarity for growth. That reset taught me to embrace the unknown, to welcome the uneasy, and to understand that the hardest decisions often carry the greatest rewards. This wasn't just the end of one chapter; it was the prologue to a story I hadn't yet imagined, filled with promise, purpose, and the undeniable power of change.

31

THE SALESMAN

Before I could sell anything to anyone, I had to sell the most important product of all: myself. Two years into my tenure at the SPACECONNECTION, the initial excitement had settled into a steady rhythm. The fires that once required constant attention had been quenched, and employee issues were under control. Yet a restlessness began to take root. I needed a new challenge, something to ignite my passion and push the company forward. That was when I turned my focus to sales—an area I believed held untapped potential.

At the time I was still serving as director of operations. My days were filled with overseeing operations, solving logistical issues, and ensuring the smooth delivery of services. It was rewarding work, but after two years it no longer felt like enough. I couldn't shake the feeling that I was capable of more—and that the company needed more of me.

The complacency gnawed at me. I'd often find myself sitting at my desk, wondering if I should start looking elsewhere. Should I jump ship and find a place where my hunger and drive would be better utilized? Or should I ride it out, waiting for the right opportunity within the company? The thoughts were relentless, but they always came back to one thing: I needed something tangible to keep up with my ambition.

One afternoon I walked into the CEO's office and laid it out. "I'm feeling restless," I admitted. "I want to do more, take on more. I need a challenge that matches my drive." To my surprise, he didn't brush me off. Instead, he leaned back in his chair and said, "Hold on. Changes are coming. Give me six to nine months." His words left me puzzled and restless. What were these changes, and more importantly, would they bring the fulfillment I was so desperately seeking? I couldn't help but wonder if waiting would lead to growth or if I was simply postponing the inevitable search for something more.

Waiting felt like an eternity. I wanted action now. But I respected his leadership and his vision for the company, so I agreed to wait—reluctantly. During that time I poured myself into finding ways to make an impact where I could. That was when I turned my attention to sales. With operations running smoothly and requiring less of my involvement, I concentrated on occasional-use sales, an area with significant potential for growth.

Occasional-use sales involve the leasing of satellite airtime on a short-term or ad hoc basis. Unlike long-term contracts, which guarantee ongoing access to satellite resources, occasional-use agreements cater to clients with temporary or event-specific needs. These clients might require airtime for a live sports broadcast for the NBA, the NFL and March Madness, breaking news coverage, or a one-off corporate event. The flexibility of occasional-use sales makes it a high-demand service, though it requires meticulous planning and quick turnaround times to accommodate unpredictable requests.

Sales had always been a natural ability for me, one rooted in my early experiences. At sixteen I worked in the shoe department at Montgomery Ward, where I discovered the thrill of helping customers find what they needed while building rapport. By eighteen I had transitioned into telemarketing, making cold calls with confidence and learning the art of persuasion. At nineteen I went door to door selling vacuum cleaners, which taught me resilience and the value of persistence in the face of rejection. These formative experiences ignited a passion for sales that never left me. I loved the challenge, the strategy, and the reward of closing a deal. One thing that always set me apart was being authentically me. Whether I was selling shoes, cold calling, or pitching vacuum cleaners, I led with honesty and genuine connection. I found that people responded to sincerity, and it became my most valuable sales tool. It was a skill I carried with me into every role, even when my job titles didn't directly involve sales.

Eventually the CEO assigned me the occasional-use sales division, which complemented the long-term contracts overseen by the sales and marketing director. The distinction in responsibilities minimized overlap, though tensions remained. Her approach leaned traditional, while I favored proactive and aggressive strategies. I made a point to include her in critical discussions, showing respect for her expertise even as I implemented my vision.

My strategy was to focus on identifying untapped opportunities and improving client relationships. By analyzing usage patterns, refining pricing models, and building stronger partnerships with clients, I was able to increase our occasional-use sales by 200 percent within a year. This growth wasn't just about numbers; it demonstrated the value of a focused and dynamic approach to sales, turning occasional-use airtime into a significant revenue stream for the company.

Seven months later the CEO called me back into his office. "You've been making waves with the sales division," he said. "It's time to expand your role." Two and a half years into my employment, I was promoted to vice president of sales and operations. The sales and marketing director became vice president of marketing, clarifying our roles and giving me the autonomy to lead all sales initiatives within the company.

The promotion wasn't just a title change. It was the culmination of months of proving my worth, demonstrating results, and showing I was ready for more responsibility. It validated my decision to stay and push for growth within the company rather than seeking opportunities elsewhere.

With my promotion, I recognized the need to build on the momentum we had achieved. I advocated for the addition of more sales staff to further develop the department and sustain our rapid growth. *Sustainability only works when you can sustain it.* Hiring new talent allowed us to expand our reach and ensure that we could meet the growing demand.

At the same time, I focused on my key strength: building and nurturing relationships. Vendor negotiations became a priority, as I worked to drive down costs and increase profitability. Strengthening these partnerships not only enhanced our bottom line but also solidified our reputation as a reliable and client-focused company. By aligning my efforts with the company's broader goals, I was able to position the sales department as a critical driver of success.

Sales taught me lessons that redefined my perspective on leadership and personal growth. First, *ambition without action is meaningless*. Asking for more responsibility—not more compensation—proved to the CEO and myself that I was invested in growth beyond personal gain. Second, leadership is not about control but about creating an environment where others can thrive. Adding talented sales staff and empowering them to excel was just as critical as hitting revenue goals. Finally, I learned the art of transforming challenges into opportunities for innovation and resilience.

Building and nurturing relationships became my cornerstone. Vendor negotiations taught me that every dollar saved was another opportunity to strengthen the company's foundation for growth. Every partnership I built was a bridge to sustainable success, reinforcing the company's reputation as an industry leader. These relationships weren't just about business; they were the cornerstone of trust. *And numbers follow trust.*

Reflecting now, I see that sales wasn't just about closing deals—it was about showing people what I stood for. Selling myself meant being more than a skilled negotiator; it meant being someone who could be trusted to deliver, time and time again. Every handshake and negotiation was proof that authenticity and results aren't mutually exclusive—they're inseparable.

32

I'M NOT READY

One year later, as I sat in the office of the CEO, I found myself at a crossroads. "What are your dreams and aspirations?" he asked. It was the kind of question that could either open doors or box you in. My heart raced as I processed the moment. Was this a test? A setup? But I leaned into the discomfort and answered honestly: "I want to continue growing this company and one day fill your shoes." His response—a simple "Great answer"—felt like a validation, but what came next floored me. "Sign this nondisclosure agreement," he said, sliding a document across the desk. My hands shook slightly as I signed.

"The time to sell the company is now," he began, explaining that the business had grown significantly in the past two years. "We have prospective buyers, and if the deal closes, we'll have a parent company, a new board of directors, and I'll stay on for two more years, and you'll be promoted to senior vice president. But I'll need you to start taking on more responsibility immediately."

Two months later the company was sold, and I stepped into my new role as senior vice president. It sounded impressive on paper, but the reality hit hard. Overnight the stakes multiplied. I wasn't just managing departments—I was shaping strategy, making decisions that affected the entire company, all while navigating the expectations of a CEO who relied on me to deliver results without excuses.

During the next two years, the CEO began his transition to retirement, and a new CEO was appointed. Whispers swirled about why I wasn't chosen to succeed him. Some thought it was politics; others believed I had been overlooked because of race. But deep down I knew my truth: I wasn't ready. Not for the weight of running an entire company. Not for the demands of leading at that level. And here's the thing—I was okay with that.

Let's be real for a moment: The thirty-one-year-old guy standing in the phone booth ten years ago—lost, jobless, and without a vision—doubted the temp job as much as he doubted himself. The weight of those years pressed heavily against the glass, daring me to take a step toward something different. Little did I know, taking that one risk would change the trajectory of my life forever.

So what does it mean to not be ready? Sometimes it's not just about self-awareness; it's also about confronting the unexpected challenges that force you to adapt and grow. I remember vividly the day we lost one of our biggest contracts because our client was acquired, and their operations were consolidated with another company. What followed was a ripple effect that left us scrambling. The consolidation created a massive utilization problem, with hundreds of hours of airtime suddenly unsold. The losses were staggering—millions of dollars per year—and there were still years remaining on the leases with our vendors. It was a perfect storm of change and uncertainty.

Technology wasn't on our side either. The rise of store-and-forward systems revolutionized syndication. It allowed syndicators to streamline their operations, cutting costs and improving efficiency. It was great for them, but for us, it left a gaping hole in our business model. We were bleeding, and the clock was ticking.

In that moment I realized that readiness isn't just about having a plan; it's also about being able to pivot when the ground beneath you shifts. It wasn't a time to freeze or dwell on the loss but a time to think critically, act decisively, and find creative ways to offset the damage. I renegotiated our leases with vendors, a move that gave us breathing room. At the same time, I went after new business opportunities to fill the gaps left by the contract loss. Bit by bit the pieces started to come together. We resolved the immediate crisis, and the company stabilized.

Even though the issues were resolved, I couldn't help but ask myself, *Am I truly ready to be 100 percent responsible for those outcomes?* I had the resilience to tackle the challenges, but did I have the confidence to carry the weight of decisions that could mean the difference between survival and failure? The one thing I hadn't considered about readiness and decision-making was the simple truth I'd proven time and time again: *There is a solution for everything.* From where my life had started to where it was now, I had defied odds and overcome challenges that would have broken many. And yet doubt still lingered, overpowering the undeniable evidence of what I had achieved. Why was it so hard to trust myself? The answer wasn't in the past; it was in embracing the weight of leadership without letting it paralyze me.

The idea of readiness is often misunderstood. People think it's a destination—a point you reach where everything clicks into place.

But readiness isn't static. It's a process. A journey. And sometimes the first step is admitting you're not there yet. For me, overcoming doubt was as much a part of that journey as solving problems or carrying responsibilities. The evidence of my successes wasn't enough to silence the doubts—they had to be faced, understood, and worked through. Readiness didn't come from waiting for doubt to disappear; it came from learning to lead with it and finding strength in what I had already proven I could overcome.

Admitting I wasn't ready turned out to be one of the most empowering decisions of my career. *It freed me from the pressure of pretending and allowed me to focus on becoming.* Readiness isn't defined by arrival; it's defined by evolution and the trust that no matter how big the challenge, there is always a solution. And that's the lesson. It's okay to not be ready. What matters is what you do with that realization.

When I stood in that phone booth all those years ago, unsure and afraid, I didn't know where that first step would take me. But I took it anyway.

33

THE PRICE OF POTENTIAL

Leadership isn't a solitary pursuit; it's a legacy shaped by those who came before us. From the earliest days of my career, mentorship has been the cornerstone of my growth. It's easy to imagine success as a straight line—a relentless climb fueled by sheer willpower. But in reality *the path to leadership is a mosaic, pieced together by the wisdom and guidance of others.* This chapter is not just about mentorship but also about how it became the catalyst for my strategic evolution as a leader.

When the new CEO arrived, I thought I was ready to prove my value. After all, I had climbed the ranks, managed large teams, and built a reputation for reliability and achieving results. But during our first one-on-one meeting, he posed a challenge that stopped me in my tracks. "You've mastered sales and operations," he said, "but now it's time to think about how all the pieces fit together. You need to see the whole board, not just your next move."

In that moment I realized that it's not about *doing* more; it's about *seeing* more. That conversation marked the beginning of a mentorship that reshaped my approach to leadership. The CEO, a highly seasoned executive with a track record of developing industry leaders, began delegating high-level responsibilities to me. At first I was overwhelmed. I had managed budgets and executed strategies before, but this was different. Now I was expected to shape the company's future—to think in terms of earnings before interest, taxes, depreciation, and amortization (EBITDA), a critical financial metric used to measure profitability and operational performance. It strips out external factors such as taxes and depreciation to give a clearer picture of a company's core earnings, enabling better strategic decision-making. Beyond this, forecasting and long-term growth became my focus rather than just day-to-day efficiency.

During one of our early meetings, the CEO addressed what everyone had been whispering about: why I wasn't chosen for the top role when the position first opened. He didn't mince words but left room for growth. "You weren't overlooked," he said. "Maybe you just weren't ready . . . yet." Those words were both humbling and motivating. *Realizing you're not at the top of your game isn't a defeat—it's a chance to level up.* The price of potential isn't just effort—it's the willingness to confront hard truths about yourself. The emotional toll of starting over and having to prove myself again was immense, but I understood that this was the cost of reaching the leader I wanted to become. *Potential demands payment in resilience, effort, and relentless self-belief.*

The CEO's guidance wasn't a standalone moment; it was part of a long chain of mentorship that had shaped my career from the start. Time and again I had crossed paths with leaders who saw something in me—potential I hadn't yet recognized in myself. Each of them left an indelible mark, building not just my skills but also my belief in what I could achieve.

I can still hear the words of my first boss when she encouraged me to apply for a supervisor role after just seven months as a full-time employee. "You're already doing the work," she said. "Why not step into the title that reflects it?" I hesitated, questioning my readiness, and she looked me in the eye and said something I'd carry for the rest of my career: "*Tear down the walls of your comfort zone before they confine your potential.*" That single moment of belief—hers in me, which sparked the belief I needed in myself—became a defining force, pushing me to silence doubts and take the leap.

Years later another mentor's challenge stretched me even further. Promoted to a management role, I was tasked with developing cost-saving strategies for satellite resources—a high-stakes assignment that demanded innovation, precision, and immediate results. Delivering on this challenge required more than skill; it demanded *accelerated learning*—a relentless pursuit of understanding and applying new knowledge at lightning speed. *The price of such growth isn't measured in hours worked but in the mental and emotional toll of constantly leveling up before you feel ready.* It's proving, again and again, that *potential is earned, not given.* These moments weren't just professional milestones; they were lessons in resilience and confidence. More importantly, they accelerated my growth, pushing me to develop faster and rise to challenges I once thought were beyond my reach.

Under the new CEO's mentorship, I underwent a transformation. At first I shadowed him during board meetings and budget reviews, observing the nuances of high-level decision-making. Gradually, he handed over the reins, challenging me to present budget proposals, lead discussions with the board, and craft our financial forecasts. Each of these responsibilities was more than a task; it was an intentional opportunity to hone my strategic thinking and refine my ability to lead under pressure.

One of the most transformative insights came during a casual conversation. "Leadership isn't about putting out fires," he said. "It's about preventing them and knowing where to build next." That statement changed the way I approached every decision. I began to connect the dots between daily operations and long-term goals, ensuring that every action contributed to a broader strategy. *Leadership is not defined by solving today's problems; it's shaped by creating tomorrow's opportunities.*

As I grew under his mentorship, I reflected on my own role as a mentor. My growth wasn't just about me; it was about creating a ripple effect. *The best leaders don't just achieve—they elevate.* I began approaching my teams with the same mindset my mentors had used with me, challenging them to stretch beyond their comfort zones, take ownership, and embrace discomfort as a catalyst for growth. *Mentorship isn't a free gift; it's an investment that demands accountability and results.* The leaders who believed in me expected a return on that belief. That expectation—that I rise to meet my potential—was the price of their guidance and the legacy I now carry forward.

If there's one thing my journey has taught me, it's this: *Growth isn't without cost.* The weight of mentorship, the expectation to rise, and the sacrifices required to unlock potential are the price every leader pays. No one rises alone.

34

THE CEO

After four years as senior vice president, the moment I had both anticipated and feared finally arrived. The CEO was departing, and I was next in line. When he asked me if I was ready to take on the role, the answer that came out of my mouth was a confident yes. But internally I wrestled with questions. Was I prepared for the immense responsibility? Could I live up to the expectations that came with leading a company at this level? My journey had prepared me in ways no training manual could, but the reality of the crown's weight was something I'd have to experience to truly understand.

The week leading up to the official announcement was a blur. Meetings, preparations, and quiet moments of reflection punctuated my days. When the call came from the board chair, inviting me to Canada to meet with him and the board, the reality hit with full force. This was no longer an audacious dream—it was happening.

The five-hour meeting with the board tested my knowledge, vision, and resilience. Every question felt like an examination of my ability to lead, but I spoke from my heart and relied on the years of experience that had brought me here. When the final question was asked, the chairman thanked me and asked if I could step out. The executive assistant escorted me to an office I could use to work while I waited. Once inside I found myself alone with my thoughts.

My hands trembled slightly as I replayed the questions, wondering if I had done enough. The hour felt like an eternity. I paced, checked my phone, and stared out the window, trying to calm my nerves. My suit felt heavier, the room hotter, and my armpits? Let's just say the deodorant was on strike, and my armpits felt like they were staging a rebellion. I seriously should have duct-taped a whole stick under each arm. Finally, two hours later, I was invited back in. As I sat down, the chairman smiled and said, "Jonathan, we believe you're the right leader for this company." Oh shit! Was this a dream come true or a nightmare fucking with me? I wondered how I managed to keep a straight face, how I stopped myself from crying right there in the boardroom. Relief, pride, fear, and determination surged through me, each emotion colliding with the other and settling into a quiet resolve.

An initial offer was made, but I wasn't pleased because it did not reflect my value. As I sat there, emotions swirled. Why were they offering me less than the two previous CEOs? Hadn't I proven myself as a major contributor to the company's success? As I sat there, I couldn't help but wonder if this was more than just a financial decision. Was this racial disparities? Did being Black factor into their calculation of my worth? It was an unsettling thought but one I couldn't dismiss entirely. I had fought my way here against odds that often seemed insurmountable, and I wasn't about to let implicit bias or systemic inequities define my value now. I knew I was the right person for the job. Years ago the impostor in me might have accepted the offer, grateful for the opportunity and feeling like someone was doing me a favor. But now I had grown—grown into someone who understood my worth and what I brought to the table. Hungry and deserving of this role, I knew settling wasn't an option.

So back to the table I went. During the negotiation, the chairman, known for his relentless focus on cost cutting, remarked, "I'm going against my instincts here, Jonathan." His comment hung in the air, but I couldn't let it pass unaddressed. I met his gaze and replied, "If I can't fight for myself, I'm not the person for this role." The room fell silent for a moment before the negotiations resumed. This wasn't just about a number on a contract—it was a defining moment of leadership, one that set the tone for how I would lead—with confidence, conviction, and an unyielding sense of my worth. After thirty minutes of back-and-forth, I accepted a deal that reflected both my contributions and the future I envisioned for the company.

POSSIBILITIES TO REALITIES

I was officially appointed president and CEO. I shook hands and was introduced to the entire executive team of the parent company. As the hours passed, I was desperately waiting for a silent moment. When I finally returned to my hotel room, I closed the door and dropped to my knees, and the emotions I had suppressed all day came rushing in. Tears welled up, and I let them fall. I cried, and I couldn't stop. They weren't tears of fear but of profound joy and gratitude.

I thought about the road I had traveled to get here—the cliffs I had scaled, the mountains I had climbed, and the hurricanes I had survived. I thought about being that ten-year-old boy, told I was the man of the house. I thought about the years spent battling addiction, the homelessness, and the countless moments when giving up seemed easier than fighting through. *I understood the probability but lived in the possibility*, pushing forward even when the odds seemed stacked against me. Yet here I was, against all odds.

After a long, restless night, I had a 6:00 a.m. flight from Ottawa, Canada, to Los Angeles. As the plane ascended, I stared out the window at the sprawling clouds, feeling a mix of exhaustion and anticipation. My mind replayed every moment of the past week, from the intense board meeting to the quiet tears in my hotel room.

This flight wasn't just a journey home; it was symbolic of my transformation. The landing in Los Angeles wasn't merely a plane touching down—it was the beginning of my leadership taking off. As the engines roared and the plane pushed through the sky, I reflected on the power of persistence, the importance of staying the course even when turbulence shakes you, and the beauty of finally reaching a higher altitude in life. This flight marked not just a return but also a new beginning.

WALKING THE TIGHTROPE

Stepping into the role of CEO felt like walking a tightrope without a safety net. There was no room for hesitation or missteps. I had reached the top, but I knew that from here, the only other place to go was out. CEOs are replaceable, and I had to ensure that I built the right foundation of support to secure both my success and the company's future.

Taking over midyear, my priority was ensuring we remained on track for the annual forecast. It was a delicate balancing act—guiding the company through ongoing operations while also positioning us for future growth. The stakes were high, and every decision carried weight, but I thrived on the challenge. Adapting to this level of responsibility required a mindset shift. There was no longer anyone to catch me, and the clarity that came with that realization sharpened my focus.

THE UNTHINKABLE

As I reflected on my journey to this moment, one milestone stood out above all others: *seven promotions in fourteen years.* Throughout my career, one thing remained constant: I always put myself in the position before I officially had it. Early on I embraced the mindset of preparing for the roles I aspired to, not just the one I held. I believed in dressing for where you want to go, not for where you are. This philosophy extended beyond clothes—it shaped how I thought, acted, and carried myself. It meant adopting the habits, the mindset, and the discipline of the person I wanted to become.

Even as a temp, I observed how managers operated, noting their decision-making, their demeanor, and their confidence. I mirrored those behaviors, not to impress anyone but to build a foundation for the leader I wanted to be. I grew into the role long before it was mine. That practice of preparation was inspired by adaptability, not just ambition. By the time the opportunities came, I wasn't just ready—I was already living them.

The story of those promotions wasn't luck or chance. It was showing up every day with a willingness to go beyond expectations, to embrace challenges as opportunities, and to lead with authenticity. Those experiences prepared me for this role, teaching me that adaptability wasn't just a skill but also the ability to evolve and thrive in any environment.

Taking on the role of CEO was not just the culmination of years of hard work—it marked the start of something greater. My vision for the company was rooted in innovation, growth, and empowerment. I wanted to create a culture where everyone felt ownership over our success, where bold ideas weren't just welcomed but expected. It was about building an organization that thrived not just on operational excellence but also on adaptability and forward thinking.

I envisioned a company that wasn't just keeping pace but setting the standard in our industry. To achieve this, I planned to invest in talent, ensuring our teams were equipped with the skills and tools needed to stay ahead of the curve. I sought to foster collaboration across every level, breaking down silos and encouraging cross-functional innovation.

But my vision wasn't limited to financial or operational goals. I wanted to lead with purpose—to show that success wasn't just about numbers on a balance sheet but also about the legacy we left behind. That meant prioritizing integrity, transparency, and a commitment to the people who made our success possible. As I began this new chapter, I knew that my greatest challenge and opportunity would be to transform this vision into reality.

35

THE BURDEN OF COMMAND

You know the old saying, "Watch what you ask for"? I wanted a career, and I got it. I wanted leadership, and I got it. I wanted to be CEO, and I got it.

Leadership, especially at the pinnacle of an organization, is often romanticized as a role of power, influence, and prestige. Yet beneath the surface lies a heavy, unspoken truth—the burden of command. As CEO, the responsibility is omnipresent, a constant companion that weighs on your shoulders, often in solitude. The decisions you make ripple outward, affecting employees, their families, and the future of the organization itself. For me, this role was both a privilege and a profound emotional toll.

THE WEIGHT OF DECISIONS

One of the most challenging aspects of being a CEO is the gravity of decision-making. Early in my tenure, I faced a gut-wrenching situation: implementing a round of layoffs. These weren't numbers on a spreadsheet; they were people I knew by name, people who had contributed to the company's growth. Sitting across from them, explaining that their roles were being eliminated, was excruciating. I carried the knowledge that while these decisions were necessary for the health of the organization, they would disrupt lives in irreversible ways. The hardest part? Walking back to my office, holding my head high while feeling the crushing weight of what I had just done.

THE LONELINESS OF LEADERSHIP

Leadership at the top can be isolating. Despite being surrounded by people, I often found myself alone in making decisions that others couldn't fully understand. Even when I had a trusted team, the ultimate responsibility rested solely on me. It was a paradox: leading a group while feeling disconnected from the camaraderie that exists among colleagues.

This isolation became most evident during times of crisis. One such moment came during a catastrophic satellite failure. Clients were furious, operations were in chaos, and the team looked to me for answers. While I had a network of advisors and technical experts, the burden of navigating the company through the storm rested on me. Success in these moments wasn't celebrated with champagne; it was greeted by exhaustion and the quiet realization that the next challenge was just around the corner.

The loneliness was compounded during my first board meeting as CEO. I vividly recall sitting in the boardroom as each member entered and took a seat on the opposite side of the long table, their expressions unreadable. It felt less like a meeting and more like an interview. Finally, the last member walked in, read the room, and chose to sit next to me—a subtle but powerful gesture.

The gravity of the moment hit me as I excused myself to the restroom to catch my breath and silence the impostor creeping into my thoughts. I had to remind myself of how I got here. Failure was not an option. That moment demanded both immense responsibility and unshakable determination—a resolve to prove I belonged in that room, leading that organization. The pressure to prove myself was immense, but so was my resolve to show them that I was the right person for the job. Those moments shaped my understanding of resilience and the importance of aligning my vision with the board's expectations. They also illuminated the inherent loneliness of leadership—the realization that, while support and mentorship can guide you, the ultimate responsibility rests solely on your shoulders. It's a solitude born from the weight of decisions, the scrutiny of your actions, and the unrelenting demand to lead with clarity and conviction, even in the face of doubt.

MANAGING RESULTS AND EXPECTATIONS

One of the more delicate challenges I faced was managing the alignment between myself and my chairman, who was the CEO of the parent company. We often clashed on priorities, particularly on how to balance immediate results with long-term sustainability. At first I would overpromise and underdeliver, leaving me in the hot seat at end-of-year board meetings. I was presenting what I thought they wanted to see rather than what was achievable with some modest stretch, effectively setting myself up for failure. It took about two budget cycles to take heed and adjust my approach. At the time I felt like a toddler learning to walk—stumbling and falling in front of an audience that wasn't shy about pointing it out. Over time I learned to stay true to my expertise and present solid, achievable goals that I could confidently deliver. This refined approach was realistic. It wasn't always the easiest approach to sell to a results-driven board. I knew, however, that building trust and credibility with stakeholders required a disciplined, strategic approach rather than missing expectations year over year.

Our differences were further amplified by circumstances beyond my control. As an employee of the subsidiary rather than the parent company, my interactions with the chairman were limited, while his other direct reports were in the same office. This dynamic created additional challenges, as I often felt I was navigating on uneven ground.

His focus was on cutting costs to increase EBITDA, frequently questioning whether my previous role as VP of sales and operations even needed to be replaced. My vision, however, was centered on growth and sustainability. I recognized that I am only one person, so why shouldn't I give myself the same opportunity to replace my previous role with someone who could support me just as I had supported previous CEOs? I deserved the same foundation for success.

The constant tension between immediate cost-saving measures and long-term investment made every decision delicate. Convincing them required data, persistence, and an unwavering belief in the strategy I had outlined.

Over time the alignment between my chairman and me began to improve, and we gradually built a great relationship founded on mutual respect and understanding. The company would go on to see positive results, meeting or exceeding expectations over the next several years. These outcomes demonstrated that balancing achievable goals with modest stretch targets could generate sustained success, even under tight scrutiny.

THE EMOTIONAL TOLL

The emotional strain of leadership is rarely discussed and always present, looming in every decision and interaction, a constant reminder of the role's weight and responsibility. As a CEO, you carry not only your own fears and doubts but also those of your team. You're the one expected to provide clarity amid uncertainty, to exude confidence even when you're questioning every decision. The weight of others' expectations can be crushing, and the emotional labor of maintaining a steady facade is exhausting.

I recall a particularly harrowing period when I had to announce the outsourcing of an entire department to the parent company's operation. The decision was strategic, aimed at ensuring the company's long-term viability, but it meant laying off employees. During an all-hands meeting, I stood in front of the team, delivering the news. The room was silent, heavy with disappointment and fear. I spent hours afterward meeting with each employee individually to advise them whether they were affected. Each conversation added another layer to the emotional burden I carried home that night.

COPING WITH THE BURDEN

To survive the weight of leadership, I had to draw deeply from my reserves of resilience, summoning strength from within to navigate the relentless demands and unexpected challenges of leadership and find ways to cope. My family became my anchor. Picking up my five-year-old son from school, taking him to the beach, and sharing an ice cream sundae became my moments of reprieve—reminders of what truly mattered and sources of much-needed perspective amid the chaos.

I also leaned on mentors who had walked this path before me. Their guidance was invaluable, offering not just practical advice but also the reassurance that I wasn't alone in feeling the weight of command. Additionally, I learned the importance of self-care—prioritizing sleep, exercise, and moments of stillness—to maintain the stamina required for the demands of the role.

LESSONS FROM THE LONELINESS

The solitude of leadership taught me invaluable lessons about empathy, authenticity, and the human side of business. Having started my career at the very bottom and worked my way up through every level of organizations, I developed a profound understanding of the challenges, pressures, and realities faced by my employees. This perspective heightened my emotional intelligence, allowing me to connect with my team and make decisions with compassion and insight. It deepened my understanding of the sacrifices made by others, from entry-level employees to fellow executives. It also shaped my leadership style, making me more attuned to the emotional and psychological needs of my team. I realized that while the burden of command is heavy, sharing its weight—through transparency, trust, and genuine connections—can lighten the load.

For those who aspire to lead, know this: Leadership is not about glory or control; it is about service. And in serving, we find purpose amid the solitude. It's making decisions that align with the organization's mission, even when they are hard. It's being the steady hand in turbulent times, the voice of reassurance when doubt is pervasive, and shouldering a burden that few will truly understand.

A LEGACY OF LEADERSHIP

Despite the challenges, I went on to serve as president and CEO of the SPACECONNECTION for thirteen years. It was a tenure defined by resilience, strategic growth, and the unwavering commitment to *balancing vision with execution.* Leadership is standing firm in the face of uncertainty, fostering a culture of trust, and ensuring that every challenge becomes a stepping stone toward growth and lasting success.

PART V

THE RETURN—LEADING FROM THE SPIRAL

I didn't survive to start over. I returned to carry forward what I fought to learn.

36

HEALING THE WEIGHT

For years I thought I had moved past my childhood. I had overcome addiction, climbed the corporate ladder, and started the journey of finding myself. On the surface it looked like I had conquered every obstacle in my path. But there was something deeper—something I hadn't fully faced. Beneath all the achievements and growth, the wounds of my childhood still lingered.

I had spent decades building a life that looked unshakable. But the truth was, I hadn't truly reckoned with the weight of my past. The pain and embarrassment of my molestation were still there, hidden behind a wall I didn't even know I had built. It wasn't until one seemingly ordinary day, sitting in the car with my brother, that everything came crashing down.

THE MOMENT OF TRUTH

My brother and I were driving, the radio playing softly in the background. We weren't paying much attention to it—just catching up, laughing about something, the way we always did. Then a story came on the news. A woman was speaking about being assaulted forty years ago and how she was just now coming forward.

At first we questioned it. Why had it taken her so long? We didn't say it outright, but there was judgment in the air. Then as I opened my mouth to say something dismissive, the words caught in my throat. I froze. The truth I had buried for decades hit me like a punch to the chest. *Damn, Jonathan. It happened to you decades ago, and you still haven't had the courage to speak up or speak out.* The pain I had avoided, the shame I had ignored, the weight I had carried—all of it came rushing forward in an instant. It wasn't the woman's story that hit me—it was mine.

SPEAKING OUT

For the first time, I spoke the words I was still too ashamed to say. I turned to my brother—my best friend, a person I trusted and respected—and said, "It happened to me too."

I didn't know what his reaction would be, but I couldn't stop. The words poured out of me—what had happened, how it made me feel, how I continued to carry it in silence all these years. He listened, his face a mix of shock, sadness, and anger—not at me but for me. When I finished, he reached over and grabbed my shoulder. "I'm sorry, bro. You're my brother," he said. "Nothing changes that. Nothing."

In that moment the weight I still carried for so long felt lighter. Speaking my truth didn't erase the pain, but it was like opening a window in a dark room. The air felt different. I could finally breathe.

ME TOO

After I told my brother, something shifted. I found myself opening up in other conversations—with another best friend, a close colleague, and eventually in quiet moments with other men I trusted. No big announcements. No drama. Just me, being real. And when I did, I kept hearing the same three words: "Me too, man."

It stopped me every time. These were men I'd respected for years—men who, like me, had built strong exteriors: fathers, husbands, leaders, providers. And yet when the door opened just a little, their pain stepped forward too. Abuse. Trauma. Shame. Stories they had buried deep and carried in silence. Some had never told a soul. Others had convinced themselves it wasn't a big deal. But as soon as I shared my truth, they felt permission to unearth theirs. And that was when I realized: *This pain wasn't rare; it was just rarely spoken.*

THE POWER OF THIS

There's a quiet revolution in those three words: "Me too, man." It's not just about validation; it's also about visibility, ending isolation, and healing the part of us that was taught to shut up and "man up." Every time one of us speaks out, it chips away at the shame that's been eating us alive. And every time someone replies, "Me too," it creates a bridge, one that leads us out of the dark.

The power of this isn't just in what we survived. It's in what we're choosing to change. I'm not sharing my story for attention. I'm sharing it for the man who's still holding his breath. For the man who thinks no one would believe him. For the man who was told real men don't cry, don't hurt, don't get abused.

Let me say it plainly: *You are not weak. You are not broken. You are not alone. You are still you. And you don't have to carry it anymore.*

ACKNOWLEDGMENT

As I worked through the memories and emotions, I began to connect with the little boy inside me—the part of me I had ignored for so long. He had been there all along, quietly carrying the weight I couldn't face.

One night during therapy, I imagined him standing in front of me. He was small, fragile, and yet so incredibly strong. His eyes met mine, filled with a mix of sadness and hope. And for the first time, I didn't look away. As tears streamed down my face, I whispered, "I see you now. You're safe. You don't have to carry this anymore." To my surprise, he stepped forward and wrapped his small arms around me. His voice, though soft, carried the weight of everything he had endured. "Thank you for seeing me again," he said. "It's been so hard carrying all the weight placed on me when my shoulders are so small. All that weight, it stunted my growth. It held us back. But now we can finally let it go."

I held him tighter as he continued, "It's time for you and me to grow into our full potential. We have so much to offer the world. Together, we can be strong, not just for us but for everyone we're meant to help."

In that moment something inside me shifted. The little boy wasn't just part of my past—he was part of my future. *He had survived so I could thrive.* And now we could finally move forward, not as two separate beings but as one.

THE WEIGHT OF HEALING

That embrace was the beginning of a new chapter. I realized that healing wasn't about erasing the past—it was about integrating it.

The little boy and I were one and the same, and his strength was now my foundation.

Every step forward was no longer just for me but also for the little boy who had carried more than he ever should have. He had waited decades for me to see him, to acknowledge his pain and his strength. Now, together, we could finally let go of the weight that had defined us for so long.

THE NEW FOUNDATION

That hug wasn't just a moment; it was a promise—a promise to honor the little boy's resilience and to use the lessons of our shared past to build a future rooted in purpose.

The weight I had carried for decades didn't disappear; it transformed, becoming the fuel for my growth, the foundation for my purpose, and the strength I would use to help others navigate their own journeys.

CHANGING BELIEFS

For so long I had been afraid to face the little boy within me. I thought his pain would be too much to bear. But in embracing him, I found the strength to let go of the weight that had held us back.

That little boy, the one who had suffered, survived, and waited patiently for me to notice him, gave me the greatest gift of all: the freedom to live fully, authentically, and purposefully.

But healing isn't a finish line; it's a journey. Even now I'm still confronting the beliefs I carried from my childhood, beliefs that no longer serve me. As a child, I was given adult responsibilities far too early, becoming a parentified child who learned to take care of myself because no one else would.

My mother was the one who instilled many of those beliefs. She told me, "You don't need to depend on anyone, not even women." She taught me to cook, clean, and manage on my own, and while those skills were practical, they came with an unspoken message: I couldn't count on others to meet my needs.

Looking back now, I understand that my mother didn't meet my emotional needs as a young child, not because she didn't love me but because she may not have known how to. Maybe it was her own upbringing, her own struggles that kept her from giving what she didn't receive herself. But I won't make excuses for her. The reality was that her actions, whether unintentional or not, reinforced the belief that I truly couldn't depend on anyone but myself. And when you believe that long enough, it becomes your truth. That belief became the armor I wore into adulthood. It felt like protection, but it also kept me isolated. If I didn't rely on anyone, I couldn't be let down. If I didn't need anyone, I couldn't be hurt. What I didn't realize then was that *independence without connection is just another form of loneliness.* Even now I catch myself carrying those beliefs into my relationships. But she wasn't the only one who shaped that belief.

THE FATHER WOUND

The father wound is a different kind of pain. For me, it didn't scream; it whispered. It wasn't loud or violent; it was quiet, passive, and constant. And that's what made it so dangerous. My father wasn't a monster or abusive, but he wasn't present either, not when it counted. Every time my mother was pregnant, he was gone. That was his pattern. When I needed stability, he was chasing his own survival. I didn't understand it then, but every time he left, he left a message behind: You're not worth staying for. That's a hell of a message for a kid to carry.

I watched him come and go, always on his own terms. And even when I did spend time with him, it was usually because I had asked. That kind of pursuit, chasing after your own father just to feel chosen, starts to etch something into your identity. You begin to wonder if the people you love will always leave. You start expecting abandonment, even from the people who claim to care about you most.

What makes this harder is that my father had a wound of his own. He didn't get what he needed either. I don't say it to excuse him; I say it because it's true. He passed on what he didn't know how to fix. And I was left trying to interpret silence, absence, and emotional distance as some version of manhood. But now I know better.

I know that fathering a child is more than biology—that's the easy part. It's about presence, protection, and showing up consistently, not conveniently. I've had to reparent myself in ways I didn't think I'd need to. I had to become the man I was searching for. The kind who stays. The kind who apologizes. The kind who doesn't run when things get hard. And even now, as I continue healing the little boy inside me and parenting my son, I carry a promise with me: The pain stops here. The father wound may have shaped me, but it doesn't define me. It's no longer my burden to pass on.

THE HEART WORK

For most of my life, I stayed in my head. That's where I felt safest—thinking through the pain, analyzing the past, controlling what I could. My heart, that part stayed guarded. I didn't even realize how much I was avoiding it until healing forced me to face it. But healing doesn't just happen in the mind. It happens in the body. In the breath. In the heart. It happens when you let yourself feel. It happens in the stillness, in the discomfort, in the moments when you want to shut down but choose to stay present instead. This kind of healing asks more from you. It asks you to feel what you've avoided.

I'm starting to recognize the signs when I begin to pull away, retreat, and go quiet. That old survival instinct kicks in, telling me to disappear, to handle it alone. But now I'm learning to do the opposite. I stay, even when my instinct is to run. This is the real work. The quiet work. The inner work. The heart work. It's not easy, but it's where the real healing lives.

Every time I choose connection over avoidance, vulnerability over silence, I feel a little more whole. I feel closer to the version of me I'm still becoming.

What's surprised me most is how healing doesn't just shift your own life; it shifts how you see everyone else too. As I started doing the heart work, I began to see my parents with new eyes. Not just for what they lacked but also for how they tried. For how they grew. And that shift gave me something I didn't expect: compassion. For them. For me. For all the broken, beautiful ways we learn to do better—eventually.

LATE LESSONS

Here's something I never saw coming: Both my parents eventually remarried and stayed in those relationships for over thirty years, until death did them part. After everything—the dysfunction, the distance, the emotional gaps they couldn't fill for each other or for me—they still found a way to get it right. Not perfect but right enough to last. Watching them build something steady later in life offered its own kind of redemption—a proof that growth doesn't always come early, but it still comes if you're willing. It showed me that transformation doesn't always happen on our timeline, but it can still happen. It taught me that people can grow, that wounds don't always define you. *That sometimes the version of you who couldn't show up in your twenties becomes the version who loves better in your fifties.* Their journey reminded me of something we all need to hear: *It's never too late to get it right. Never too late to love better. Never too late to change.*

The little boy within me reminds me every day, "We're still growing. We're still learning. And that's okay." As we stand together, no longer separate, I whisper to him all the time, "We've got this. Together, we've got this."

If you're ready, think of someone who caused you deep pain. Now think of one moment when you caused pain (we all have). What would healing look like on both sides?

37

THE 360 DEGREES OF RESILIENCE

Resilience isn't a moment; it's a movement. But it's not a circle. It's a spiral. Most people think resilience is about bouncing back. They treat it like a skill you turn on after life knocks you down. But resilience isn't one-dimensional. It's emotional, mental, relational, physical, strategic, and professional. It's not something I learned in theory. It's something I lived—and nearly died through.

For years I kept breaking in the same places. Same emotional cracks. Same relational triggers. Same leadership struggles. And I couldn't figure out why I couldn't just "get over it." What I needed couldn't be found in a quote. I needed something that could hold all of it—my failures, my fears, my fight to keep going. I didn't know it then, but I was already living it.

I didn't set out to create a framework. But when I looked back—at the breakdowns, the pivots, and the returns—I saw a pattern: the spiral. I had been living it long before I could name it. The 360 Degrees of Resilience didn't come after the transformation. It was the transformation.

This isn't some whiteboard brainstorm. This is how I survived trauma, addiction, fatherhood, failure, leadership, grief, and success and still kept going. This is the system that carried me from tested to trusted to transformational.

THE SPIRAL CONCEPT

Many times, 360 degrees means you end up where you started. But when I say 360, I don't mean a flat loop. I mean a spiral, an upward climb. You return to familiar places: the pain, the past, the people, the titles you outgrew, the failed businesses. But this time you show up with new truth. More healing. More power. Wisdom where there was once reaction, strength that was once survival, and a purpose shaped by the shit you walked through.

The spiral has four movements.

1. Recognition (Descent)—Life cracks you open—through burnout, failure, misalignment, identity crisis, or resurfacing grief. You begin to see what's really underneath.
2. Reckoning (Stillness)—You stop running. You sit with the truth. You stop surviving long enough to start processing, and healing.
3. Reframing (Ascent)—You give your story new meaning. You rise from the same place—but not as the same person, the same team, the same leader.
4. Rebirth (Expansion)—You move forward with purpose, not just progress. Your past becomes your platform.

Each movement of the spiral doesn't take you back; it takes you deeper. With every turn, you rise with more perspective, more ownership, and more strength. That's what makes it a spiral—not a circle. You're not just rising; you're also elevating with intention. Every turn gives you altitude and authority. Every stage of my life—personal, professional, and everything in between—was marked by one of these four dimensions of resilience. Each spiral built the next version of me.

The first spiral: the root, the war within.

EMOTIONAL AND MENTAL RESILIENCE

You've read my story. You know I didn't just face pain; I carried it. Shame, abandonment, addiction, loss. And none of that goes away by pretending it didn't happen. It only heals when you confront it with honesty and intention.

This level of resilience is about the stuff behind the scenes. The inner war that nobody claps for. Therapy. Self-talk. Prayer. Pattern-breaking. It's how you make peace with your past while still building your future. *You don't build resilience by pretending it doesn't hurt. You build it by learning how to heal while you lead.*

I remember lying in that hospital bed after pretending to swallow a bottle of sleeping pills. Liquid charcoal dripping from my mouth and leaking from my ass. Nurses shouting, "Stay with us, Jonathan!" Machines beeping like a countdown clock. I wasn't dying from drugs; I was suffocating from everything I hadn't dealt with. Shame. Guilt. Unworthiness. All the stuff I thought I could outrun.

As I lay in the psych ward listening to my roommate talk to people who weren't there, I wasn't just scared of him; I was also scared of me. Scared of how far I had spiraled with no tools, no mirror, no plan. Looking back, I realized resilience doesn't start with a second chance. It starts with a second look, inward. "How did I get here?"

The second spiral: where your pain meets people.

RELATIONAL AND CULTURAL RESILIENCE

I had to relearn connection. Rebuild trust. Reconcile with people I hurt. I couldn't keep dragging my emotional baggage into every room. That included my family, my marriage, and my leadership teams. And when I entered corporate spaces, I had to navigate cultures that weren't built for someone like me. I didn't just have to survive the room—I had to change it. *You don't just inherit culture. You shape it. You challenge it. You lead it forward.*

This spiral taught me how to show up without shrinking and how to stop letting pain speak before I did.

I'll never forget the time a guest accused me of stealing from her wallet while working the front desk of the hotel. I was well liked and high performing. And still, all it took was her finger pointing in my direction and saying, "The Black man stole my money," to erase all of that. No evidence. No conversation. Just accusation. I stood there, frozen. Not because I had done something wrong but because I had been here before. And here I was again—same story, different uniform. I didn't just have to defend myself. I had to defend my dignity.

Resilience means choosing your identity over their assumptions. It's confronting the version of yourself that others project onto you and deciding who you're going to be regardless of their limitations.

The third spiral: the growth lane.

STRATEGIC AND ADAPTIVE RESILIENCE

Going from temp to CEO in just fourteen years, with seven promotions along the way, didn't happen because I hustled harder. It happened because I learned how to read rooms, shift plans, and adjust with purpose. This level of resilience is about clarity, not chaos. Strategy, not survival. It's having a plan and the power to pivot when that plan explodes. *The kind of resilience that sustains leadership isn't reactive. It's prepared. Strategic. Nimble. It's having a blueprint that adjusts with the wind but keeps moving toward the mission.*

When I was a temp, I thought hard work would be enough. But I quickly learned that navigating leadership wasn't just about performance; it was about positioning. Reading the room. Knowing when to speak, when to move, and when to shift the blueprint without losing the foundation.

One moment that I was tested was when we lost a major partner because of circumstances beyond my control. Everything we'd built around that deal started to collapse. But instead of panicking, I restructured the offer, repitched the vision, and rebuilt the team's belief before I rebuilt the revenue. Strategy wasn't just the tool. It was the lifeline. *Resilience at this level isn't about surviving the fall; it's about preparing for the pivot.*

The fourth spiral: the core, the anchor, the nonnegotiable.

IDENTITY-BASED RESILIENCE

All the other spirals collapse without this one. This isn't about the role I played at work or the mask I wore at home. This is about who I chose to become when no one else was watching. This is where legacy lives. I didn't escape my past. I integrated it. I used every loss as leverage, every scar as strategy, and every broken place as part of the blueprint.

You remember the story—the red train set I got for Christmas. What stayed with me long after the wrapping paper and the tears was this truth: That little boy never stopped needing me.

It's also what shows up in the moments that test your integrity. Like when you walk away from a leadership role or a promotion, not because you couldn't take it but because it would've required you to betray who you are. That's when your values speak louder than your title. *Identity-based resilience is what happens when you stop waiting to be saved and start showing up for the version of yourself that needed you most.*

THIS ISN'T A LOOP; IT'S A CLIMB

This wasn't about escaping my past. It was about reclaiming every part of it. The 360 wasn't a process I designed—it was my life. It was the shape my growth took. Each return wasn't a repeat—it was a rise. With more clarity. More courage. More alignment. *Resilience means facing the fire again, with the strength to stand in it and the wisdom to walk through it.*

THE SPIRAL IN MOTION; WHEN THE WORK MEETS THE WORLD

Resilience doesn't end when you heal—it begins again when you lead. The spiral expands when you become responsible for more than your own life. That's where I found the test—and the truth—of everything I had built. Because resilience in leadership isn't about showing strength. It's *holding* strength. It's being able to manage energy—yours and others'—so that the spiral doesn't collapse under pressure. I had to learn how to lead through exhaustion without letting burnout set the tone. I had to manage momentum—keeping teams moving forward when everything around them was trying to pull them back.

Leading from the spiral meant owning my emotional gravity. People didn't just follow my words—they followed my energy, my alignment, my pace. And when I was out of sync, everything else slipped too.

Every level of the spiral showed up again in my leadership. Emotional resilience became empathy in hard conversations. Relational resilience became culture-building in broken teams. Strategic resilience became clarity in chaos. Identity resilience became the compass when I had to walk away from deals, partnerships, or titles that didn't align with who I had become. The spiral wasn't just for me anymore—it became the system I led from.

Most people stop at 180, just far enough to turn their back on what broke them. But that's only half the journey. I made the full turn, the full 360. I faced it all, owned every part of it, and used it to lead forward. This wasn't about healing once. It was about evolving continuously—layer by layer, version by version. That's the real climb.

I stopped asking, "Why did this happen to me?" and started asking, "What did it create in me?" This is the shift that broke the cycle of reactive survival and built a rhythm of proactive transformation. Whether you're leading a company, recovering from loss, or building yourself from the ground up, this isn't just a story. It's a strategy.

38

ODDS GET BEAT

I wasn't supposed to make it. Let's start there. Not with a motivational quote. Not with a warm-up story. Just the truth. I wasn't supposed to survive the streets. I wasn't supposed to recover. I wasn't supposed to make it out of addiction, depression, or poverty. I wasn't supposed to become a father who breaks cycles instead of continuing them. I wasn't supposed to lead anyone—let alone become a board-appointed CEO. The odds were stacked like bricks on my chest, and every breath felt borrowed. But here I am.

MIC DROP

Let me break it down for you. I understood the *probability.* I just chose to live in the possibility. *Probability is a prediction. Possibility is a decision.* That's the real game changer. That's what separates the stuck from the unstuck, the dreamers from the doers, the survivors from the builders. Living in possibility means refusing to believe the story that stats wrote for you.

Let's be real. There was nothing about my circumstances that screamed success. And when I did start to win, I still heard whispers that it wouldn't last. That I wasn't ready. That I was just lucky. That the mask would fall off and expose the broken kid underneath. Here's the thing: *The broken kid never disappeared. I just stopped letting him drive.* That's survival wisdom. That's resilience. *You don't have to erase who you were to become who you are.* I carried every version of me—scared, angry, reckless, hopeful—into this moment. And together, we built a life I wasn't supposed to have.

The statistics never measured hunger. Real hunger. The kind that burns through excuses, fear, and comfort zones. The kind that shows up when nobody else will. The kind that makes you rise when you've got nothing left but faith and fumes. They don't measure that kind of hunger because they can't. It's untrackable. Unteachable. But if you've ever had it, you know it. You know what it means to grind—not for Instagram, not for applause but for rent, for food, for dignity. You know what it means to sit in silence while your soul screams for more. You know what it means to be counted out but refuse to stay down.

The odds didn't get beat by luck. They got beat by work. Grit. Grace. Strategy. And a whole lot of stubborn faith. Sometimes survival means tricking yourself into thinking you've already won just to get through another day. Sometimes it means standing up with shaking knees and saying, "Let's go again." The odds don't know your heart. They don't know your hustle. They don't know why you keep showing up. They don't know your why. But you do. And that's all you need.

Statistically speaking I should've been a headline, not an author. But the odds don't know who they're dealing with when they come for somebody with nothing to lose and everything to prove. *They measured my risk, but they couldn't quantify my resilience. They saw the struggle but missed the strategy. They counted the scars but never calculated the comeback.* And that's where the odds got it wrong. Beating the odds isn't loud. It's silent. *It's the moment you pick purpose over pride. Discipline over drama. Faith over fear.*

You want to know how the odds got beat? *I didn't look for a finish line—I looked for momentum.* I stacked small wins like bricks. I failed forward. I burned the blueprint and built my own. Every boardroom I entered, every table I sat at, I brought all versions of me with me. Not to hide them but to honor them. Because without the street-smart kid, the broken brother, the temp who got overlooked, I wouldn't be the man standing here. *You don't have to erase your past to earn your future.* That's the lie the world sells. And here's the part they don't teach you: The past is the foundation, and I used every mistake as mortar. Every loss became leverage.

I've been invisible in boardrooms and loud in rehab. I've been underestimated, overlooked, and counted out more times than I can count. I've walked through hell with my shoelaces untied, praying I didn't trip. But even then I fell forward. You choose to keep showing up. To keep healing. To keep building. Even when you're tired. Even when it doesn't make sense. Even when it feels like no one's watching.

Let this chapter be your permission slip to ignore the stats. You're not a trend. You're not a percentage. You're not a footnote in someone else's report. *You are the proof that resilience doesn't ask permission.*

So here's the real secret: The odds get beat the moment you stop trying to fit into the life they told you you'd have and start building the one you were born to lead. *The most powerful mindset you can have isn't proving them wrong. It's proving yourself right.*

Next move: Make a list titled: "The Things That Tried to Stop Me."

Write down every fear, failure, doubt, label, person, or moment that made you question if you'd keep going. Now draw a bold line underneath it all—and write:

"I'm still here. And I get to decide what happens next."

IF YOU'RE STRUGGLING

I've stood at the edge. Overwhelmed. Addicted. Ready to quit life altogether. I've felt the kind of pain that doesn't just hurt—it convinces you the world would be better off without you. But I'm still here. Not because I had all the answers. Not because I was stronger than the struggle. I'm here because I reached out—eventually—and someone answered.

If you're reading this and you're in a dark place, please hear me: This is not your ending. There is help. There is healing. And there is a version of you still waiting to be discovered. Don't do it alone. There's a lifeline waiting.

GET HELP NOW

Suicide & Crisis Lifeline (24/7)

- Dial 988
- 988Lifeline.org

Substance Abuse and Mental Health Services Administration (SAMHSA)

- 1-800-662-HELP (4357)
- SAMHSA.gov

Crisis Text Line

- Text **HELLO** to **741741**
- CrisisTextLine.org

The Trevor Project (LGBTQ+ Youth Support)

- 1-866-488-7386
- TheTrevorProject.org

Veterans Crisis Line

- Dial **988**, then press **1**
- VeteransCrisisLine.net

You don't have to explain your pain to be worthy of healing. You just have to survive today.

—Jonathan Crawford, *Recovering addict, survivor, and proof that it's possible*

THE PTG PHENOMENON

Revolutionizing our understanding of recovery, psychologists Richard G. Tedeschi and Lawrence G. Calhoun first introduced the concept of post-traumatic growth (PTG) in the mid-1990s. Their groundbreaking work, especially through the seminal book *Posttraumatic Growth: Conceptual Foundations and Empirical Evidence*, explores the profound transformation individuals can undergo following traumatic experiences. This foundational research not only established PTG but also paved the way for the exploration of "transformation through trauma," illustrating how adversity can lead to remarkable personal growth.

PTG highlights a profound, positive transformation that some individuals experience after facing major life crises or traumatic events. This concept extends beyond merely bouncing back; it's about a deep, meaningful change where people can find themselves feeling stronger and more fulfilled than before their trauma experiences. It reveals how challenges can become catalysts for personal growth, leading to deeper life appreciation and stronger human connections. When trauma disrupts your life, it shatters your previous understanding of the world, pushing you into a realm of new, often harsh realities. This confrontation with trauma is not just about managing adversity; it's an opportunity to reconstruct your life with a new lens, often reevaluating what really matters.

As survivors navigate through their emotional aftermath, they often uncover strengths they didn't realize they had. This newfound resilience can be empowering, underscoring the transformation through trauma as not just a recovery but also a rebirth of sorts. Handling intense emotions becomes a crucial skill, part of why many emerge from trauma feeling more capable and robust. Deepening relationships is another significant aspect of this transformation. There's a profound understanding and empathy that develops among those who've faced similar trials, fostering supportive, meaningful bonds. Moreover, trauma often nudges people to venture into uncharted territories—whether it's a new career, a hobby, or a rekindled passion—adding vibrant new chapters to their life stories. Many also experience a renewed appreciation for the simple joys of life. What was once mundane now holds special significance, a common theme among those who undergo transformation through trauma. Some find their experiences leading to deep spiritual revelations or shifts in their belief systems, further enriching their personal evolution.

The path from trauma to growth isn't about returning to a previous state; it's about forging ahead with a richer, more complex understanding of life. This transformation involves rethinking one's beliefs and values, learning to manage emotions more effectively, and finding meaning in the trauma, which often reshapes one's purpose and priorities. Tools such as the Posttraumatic Growth Inventory help measure this growth, providing insights not just for academic purposes but also for practical support in therapy and recovery. These tools assist therapists and survivors alike in understanding the extent of transformation and in navigating the ongoing journey of recovery.

The concept of transformation through trauma offers an uplifting view of human resilience and potential. It illustrates how, even after devastating events, there is a pathway not just to recovery but also to profound personal growth and fulfillment. While PTG is not a universal outcome, for those who experience it, it marks a significant transformation toward living a more enriched and meaningful life. This understanding helps us appreciate the complex yet beautiful ways people adapt and evolve through their most challenging experiences.

THE CRACK WAVE

In the early 1980s, Los Angeles and various other prominent American cities witnessed the emergence of a novel drug: crack cocaine. Crack, so named for the crackling sound it made while smoking it, was a highly potent and smokable variant of cocaine that quickly grew in popularity because of its affordability and ease of production. Only a decade or two earlier, cocaine itself was the attractive party drug of choice, primarily snorted by the rich and famous because of its steep cost. Crack's rapid adoption, particularly in impoverished urban areas, marked a significant departure from the 1970s glam drug, thus paving the way for numerous social, economic, and public health problems that are still felt to this day.

Los Angeles became a focal point for the distribution of crack cocaine, largely because of its location, the extensive highway network, and the presence of various street gangs. The rise of crack provided these gangs with a new, highly lucrative source of income, which exacerbated gang violence and crime rates in the city. The epidemic took a devastating toll on the social fabric of the city. It ravaged communities, destroyed families, and caused a significant increase in addiction rates, overdose deaths, and crime. The socioeconomic disparities within the city grew even wider beyond the already-affected marginalized and impoverished neighborhoods.

Law enforcement and judicial response to the epidemic were also fraught with controversy. In 1986 the war on drugs, initiated by the Reagan administration, led to a new legislation that established minimum sentencing laws for crack cocaine possession and distribution. Under this law, possessing just five grams of crack mandated a minimum five-year sentence, while possessing fifty grams required a ten-year minimum sentence. In comparison an individual with powdered cocaine would need one hundred times as much to incur equal penalty. These new laws were justified by baseless claims that crack was more addictive than its parent drug, cocaine. African American and Latino communities became primary targets, leading to a dramatic increase in incarceration rates among the populations. This further stigmatized and strained these communities, creating a vicious cycle of poverty, crime, and imprisonment. In addition the health-care system was ill-prepared to deal with the health consequences of widespread crack use. Treatment facilities couldn't meet the rising demand, and many addicts did not have access to the necessary health care because of their socioeconomic constraints.

Since the peak of the epidemic, there has been a reassessment of the crisis response, placing greater emphasis on treating drug addiction as a public health concern rather than exclusively as a criminal matter. Nevertheless, the repercussions of the 1980s crack epidemic persist. The widespread imprisonment of minority populations, the heightened impoverishment and marginalization of already vulnerable communities, and the aggravation of public health challenges, among other consequences, continue to echo throughout American society. Exploring the 1980s crack epidemic provides a crucial perspective on the intersection of drug policy, socioeconomic inequality, and systemic racism in the United States. It constitutes a significant, albeit painful, chapter in our history that imparts essential lessons for tackling similar issues in the future.

ACKNOWLEDGMENTS

This book took six years, emotional tears, and quiet spaces to relive a journey I spent years trying to outrun. But the story had to be told. Because some truths don't heal until they're heard—fully, freely, and without apology.

To my son, Jonathan—you now hold my truth in your hands. The full truth of who I was, what I faced, and what I overcame. This book is my voice, and now it's yours to hear. Every page is proof of what's possible. May it give you clarity, courage, and conviction for every mountain you face. Because where we start never defines how far we can go.

To my sister, Mirian—you were the light that broke me open, the one who saw me, shaped me, and unknowingly started my journey toward healing. From the days you walked me home hand in hand, braided my hair, and showed me how to carry myself with confidence, you were teaching me how to see myself when the world refused to. You weren't just creative, brilliant, and accomplished—you were a presence. Your humility, your art, your laughter … they stayed with me long after you left the room. And that final lunch? I carry your words with me still. You told me you were proud. You told me to take care of myself. I thought we were building an adult bond. I didn't know we were saying goodbye. Your passing shattered something in me. But it also cracked open the silence I had lived in for too long. You lit the spark that became my path to self-awareness, growth, and truth. This book is my voice—and in so many ways, it's yours too. We never got to heal together. But I hope these pages begin what we never got to finish. I carry your light, always.

To my mother—you were small in stature but unshakable in spirit. My earliest example of strength. You solved problems with grit and grace, even when life gave you more than your share of hardship. But there was another side to you, too—the woman who walked the runway at fashion shows while I deejayed. You had style, elegance, and a quiet confidence that lit up every room you entered. Watching you do your thing while I played music are memories I still cherish. You were the youngest eighty-year-old woman I've ever known—sharp, stylish, and full of fire. We carried some things in silence, but what we built was a bond forged through struggle, love, and resilience. You lived eighty-eight years with purpose in your step and fire in your voice. The respect your family had for you said everything. It was an honor to be your son. I wish you were here to hold this book in your hands—but I feel your presence on every page.

To my pops—you lived eighty-six full years, and every one of them left a mark. You didn't just tell stories—you preached them like sermons, wrapped in wisdom and laced with lessons. I still hear your voice in mine. And yes, you left me your gray hair too—wisdom, wisdom. I see you in all your children. The legacy you left is written in how we carry ourselves, in the respect we command, and in the Crawford name we all cherish. With your grandkids, that legacy stretches even further. You gave us more than memories—you gave us a blueprint. You held true to who you were in every room you entered—never chasing approval, never bending to fit the moment. You moved with conviction and carried yourself with humility and strength. Everyone respected you. Everyone felt your presence. I watched you grow into a man others looked up to, and I know you'd be proud of who I've become—just like you always made me feel throughout my journey. Your words still guide me. Your presence still grounds me. Thank you for giving me a name, a legacy, and a standard to live by.

To Jonas L.—my brother and best friend. Thirteen years between us didn't matter. We were locked in from day one. I remember standing in the front seat of the car while you were driving, looking up at you like you were everything. And you were. You introduced me to music, to confidence, and to a version of cool I couldn't wait to grow into. You're the reason I rocked the shag cut and Jheri curl for years—thank you for that boost. You had style, soul, and this contagious energy that made people want to be around you. Our relationship evolved over the years, but one thing never changed: we were solid. I miss those early-morning phone calls on my way to the office. I miss the laughs. Like the time a waitress asked if you were my dad—we cracked up about that for weeks. You had a way of bringing humor into every situation, even the hard ones. And in the wild moments and my newsworthy stories, your catchphrase always came through—"Hold up, let me get my popcorn." I still hear your laugh. I still feel the void. And I still wish you were here to read the full story. I miss our shit-talking. I miss you.

To Gregory, my brother—always the strategist. I was just six when we played those chess games, not realizing you were teaching me how to think critically, plan ahead, and see the bigger picture—lessons that shaped how I move through life. But you gave me more than strategy. You gave me presence. From Navy-leave trips to jazz concerts and Magic Mountain, you never showed up halfway. I never once saw you angry. Your voice carried calm, and your spirit carried grace. You were the kind of man whose strength didn't shout—it settled in. Watching you refuse painkillers at the end, holding tight to your faith, showed me a level of courage that changed me. I'm grateful for the love and respect we shared—for each other, and for our mother. Thank you for the quiet power you walked in every day of your life.

To my sister Connie—watching you grow into yourself was a gift I'll never forget. You lived with quiet bravery, always willing to give your last, even when you had so little left for yourself. You showed up for others through your own storms, never asking for recognition, just wanting to make things easier for everyone else. That kind of grace doesn't disappear—it lives on. I saw your strength in those final years, but more importantly, I saw your spirit rise. We found our way back to each other, and I'm proud of the woman you became. Thank you for showing me what love looks like when it costs you something.

To Alexis Roth, the mentor who took me under her wing—the person who hired the temp and trained me to replace you one day. You saw something in me long before I could see it myself. From encouraging me to apply for my first supervisory position to later working beside me as a colleague—thank you for believing in me every step of the way.

Robert (Bob) Patterson—what a journey. Thank you for trusting me, for giving me space to grow, and for opening doors that changed the trajectory of my life. When I told you I wanted to fill your shoes one day, your response gave me hope—and that hope helped carry me forward.

To the mentors who shaped me, so many to name—thank you for seeing beyond the surface. Your guidance wasn't always easy to hear, but it was exactly what I needed. You challenged my thinking, stretched my vision, and refused to let me settle for less than the truth.

To everyone who ever heard a piece of my story and said, "You need to write a book"—this is for you. You planted the seed long before I had the courage to water it.

To the readers—the survivors, the ones still trying, the ones navigating with no clear path forward—this is for you.

To those who didn't survive—your story still matters. Your struggle wasn't weakness. It was real, it was heavy, and it deserves to be honored.

For the families who lost someone to addiction, depression, and were left asking why. For the codependent who carried someone else's pain until they lost sight of their own. You are seen.

We don't all make it through. But those of us who do have a responsibility—not just to survive, but to tell the truth about how we did. This is mine.

ABOUT THE AUTHOR

Jonathan Crawford is an executive leader, keynote speaker, and resilience strategist who turned adversity into authority. Today, he helps organizations and individuals navigate growth, sustainability, and change. Over the past two decades, Jonathan has built a legacy of leadership—delivering results, driving transformation, and developing people at every level.

Resilience isn't just what Jonathan does—it's who he became, so others could believe they can too. His story is not about perfection; it's persistence, and helping others find the strength to keep going when life gets uncertain or unrelenting. For Jonathan, joy fuels growth—and growth builds legacy. That's the work he lives for.

He is president of Broadcast and Media in the telecommunication industry, the CEO of Source Link Media, and a certified coach in disruption, transformation, leadership, and resilience. His career began in a temporary role and accelerated through seven promotions in fourteen years to become a board-appointed CEO. While the titles marked his rise, it was the transformation that defined him. It is Jonathan's belief that titles follow impact, and transformation begins when you trade the performance for presence.

At one point, his life was spiraling—personally, emotionally, and professionally. He knows what it's like to question your worth, feel stuck in a season, or struggle to find a way forward. Along the way, he didn't just grow in title—he grew in depth. Jonathan's real expertise goes beyond leading teams—it's in rebuilding a life that works from the inside out.

Today, Jonathan uses every part of that journey to speak, coach, mentor, and guide others through their own turning points. Whether it's resilience, reinvention, recovery, or high-performance transformation, he shows that winning means more when you don't lose yourself getting there. The real victory is rising with your integrity intact.

Beyond the stage and boardroom, Jonathan is driven by the joy of being a dad, sharing laughter with loved ones, and showing up for the people who matter most. That's the part of his life that keeps him grounded, grateful, and whole. He brings the same passion, energy, and belief to every space he enters; joy is a strategy—not just a feeling.

in mrjonathancrawford
X jonathancrawf